Fuel Your Dreams:

A Guide to Fueling Entrepreneurship

© 2023 Ehsan Zarrini
Layout and Cover: Books on Demand
Publisher: BoD – Books on Demand, Helsinki, Finland
Manufacturer: BoD – Books on Demand, Norderstedt, Germany
ISBN: 978-952-80-0062-4

Fuel Your Dreams:

A Guide to Fueling Entrepreneurship

To my dearest Sima and all the inspirations in my life,

It is with immense gratitude and joy that I present to you my book, "Fuel Your Dream: A Guide to Fueling Entrepreneurship." This book is the product of countless hours of hard work, dedication, and perseverance. And I could not have done it without the support and encouragement of so many amazing people in my life.

First and foremost, I want to thank my love, Sima. Your unwavering belief in me and my dreams has been my greatest source of inspiration. You have always been there for me, cheering me on, and pushing me to be my best self. I am grateful for your love and support every day, and I dedicate this book to you.

I also want to extend my deepest thanks to all the people who have inspired me along the way. To my family and friends who have always been there for me, thank you for your unwavering support and encouragement. To the entrepreneurs and business leaders who have shared their insights and wisdom with me, thank you for your generosity and inspiration. And to all the people who have believed in me, even when I didn't believe in myself, thank you for your faith and encouragement.

This book is a testament to the power of dreams, hard work, and perseverance. It is my hope that it will inspire and empower others to pursue their own dreams, just as I have been inspired and empowered by so many amazing people in my life.

With love and gratitude,

Ehsan

Welcome to "Fuel Your Dreams: A Guide to Fueling Entrepreneurship." Whether you are a seasoned entrepreneur or just starting out, this comprehensive and practical guide will equip you with the knowledge and tools necessary to turn your dreams into reality.

Authored by expert in the field of entrepreneurship, "Fuel Your Dreams" is packed with real-world case studies, insights, and actionable strategies that have helped successful entrepreneurs launch and grow their ventures. From ideation and market analysis to funding and scaling, this book provides readers with a clear roadmap to navigate the entrepreneurial landscape.

Through a step-by-step approach, "Fuel Your Dreams" empowers readers to overcome common obstacles and achieve their goals. Whether you need guidance on identifying your target market, developing a strong brand, or leveraging digital marketing, this book covers all aspects of entrepreneurship.

With "Fuel Your Dreams," you will gain the confidence and skills needed to build a sustainable and thriving business in today's competitive landscape. So, take the first step towards fueling your dreams and dive into this invaluable resource.

Index

Introduction to Entrepreneurship
- Definition and Explanation of Entrepreneurship
- Key Characteristics of Entrepreneurs
- Benefits of Being an Entrepreneur
- Pivoting and making key decisions
- The art of pivoting
- Entrepreneurial Mindset and Habits

Identifying and Validating Your Business Idea
- Conducting Market Research
- Identifying Your Target Market
- Evaluating the Feasibility of Your Business Idea

Developing a Business Plan
- Understanding the Importance of a Business Plan
- Key Components of a Business Plan
- Setting Realistic Goals and Objectives

Securing Funding and Investment
- Understanding Your Funding Options
- Preparing a Pitch Deck
- Networking with Investors
- Crowdfunding and Alternative Funding Sources

Building a Strong Team
- Importance of Building a Strong Team
- Hiring and Managing Employees
- Building a Culture of Collaboration and Innovation
- Building a Diverse and Inclusive Business: Strategies for Entrepreneurs

Marketing and Branding
- Understanding the Importance of Marketing
- Developing a Marketing Strategy
- Building a Strong Brand Identity
- Building a Strong Online Presence

Managing Your Finances
- Understanding Financial Statements
- Budgeting and Cash Flow Management
- Managing Taxation and Legal Requirements

Navigating Challenges and Overcoming Obstacles
- Common Challenges Faced by Entrepreneurs
- Developing Resilience and Adaptability
- Seeking Support and Mentorship
- Entrepreneurial Burnout and Self-Care
- Time Management and Productivity

Scaling and Growing Your Business
- Understanding the Stages of Business Growth
- Identifying Opportunities for Expansion
- Building a Sustainable Business Model
- Strategic Partnerships and Alliances
- International Expansion and Global Markets

Leveraging Technology for Your Business
- Understanding the Role of Technology in Business
- Identifying Technologies that can Benefit Your Business
- Implementing and Managing Technology Solutions

Innovative and Sustainable Business Practices
- Importance of sustainable practices
- Implementing Innovative and Sustainable Business
- Overcoming the Challenges of Implementing Innovative and Sustainable Business

Balancing Work and Life as an Entrepreneur
- Understanding the Importance of Work-Life Balance
- Strategies for Managing Work and Personal Life
- Developing Habits for Maintaining Well-being and Health

Ethics and Social Responsibility in Entrepreneurship
- Understanding the Role of Ethics and Social Responsibility in Business
- Identifying Ethical and Social Responsibilities in Your Business
- Incorporating Ethics and Social Responsibility into Your Business Practices

Conclusion and Final Thoughts
- Reflecting on Your Entrepreneurial Journey
- Celebrating Your Accomplishments
- Encouraging Continued Learning and Growth

Introduction to Entrepreneurship

Entrepreneurship is a dynamic and exciting field that offers individuals the opportunity to turn their creative ideas and innovative solutions into successful businesses. Entrepreneurs are individuals who start and run their own businesses, taking on the risk and reward of their ventures. Entrepreneurship is a process that involves identifying an opportunity, developing a business plan, securing funding, building a team, and scaling and growing the business.

In this book, "Fuel Your Dreams: A Guide to Fueling Entrepreneurship," we will explore the key elements of entrepreneurship, from identifying and validating a business idea to building a successful and sustainable business model. Whether you are just starting out or looking to grow your existing business, this guide will provide you with the tools, strategies, and knowledge to fuel your entrepreneurial journey and achieve your goals.

So, what exactly is entrepreneurship? Simply put, entrepreneurship is the process of starting and running a business, from concept to commercialization. It is a journey of self-discovery, growth, and learning, and requires a combination of creativity, passion, determination, and hard work. Whether you are looking to start a new business, grow an existing one, or pivot to a new opportunity, entrepreneurship provides you with the platform to make your dreams a reality.

Definition and Explanation of Entrepreneurship

Entrepreneurship can be defined as the process of creating or starting a new business venture with the aim of making a profit. It involves identifying a need in the market, developing a business idea to meet that need, and taking the necessary steps to bring the idea to life, such as securing funding, building a team, and marketing the product or service.

Entrepreneurs are individuals who take on this process, often taking on significant risk and uncertainty in pursuit of their vision. They are typically driven by a passion for their idea and a desire to bring it to the market. They are often creative, innovative, and able to think outside the box in order to find new and better solutions to problems.

Entrepreneurship can also refer to the mindset and approach that entrepreneurs bring to their business and personal lives. This mindset is characterized by a willingness to take calculated risks, a focus on problem-solving, and a desire for continuous improvement and growth.

In summary, entrepreneurship can be seen as a combination of creativity, innovation, and risk-taking, aimed at creating new and better solutions to problems in the market, with the ultimate goal of making a profit.

Key Characteristics of Entrepreneurs

Entrepreneurs are a unique breed of individuals who possess certain characteristics that help them succeed in their business ventures. Some of the key characteristics of entrepreneurs include:

- Risk-taking: Entrepreneurs are often willing to take calculated risks in order to bring their vision to life. They are not afraid to try new things and embrace failure as a learning opportunity.
- Innovation: Entrepreneurs are known for their ability to think creatively and find new and better solutions to problems. They are often at the forefront of new trends and technologies and are not afraid to challenge the status quo.
- Determination: Entrepreneurs are highly motivated and driven individuals who are not easily discouraged. They are often willing to put in long hours and make sacrifices in order to reach their goals.
- Adaptability: Entrepreneurs must be able to adapt to changes in the market, customer needs, and other factors that can impact their business. They are often able to quickly pivot and adjust their strategy in response to changing circumstances.
- Self-motivation: Entrepreneurs are often highly self-motivated and able to work independently. They are driven by their passion for their idea and their desire to bring it to the market.
- Networking: Entrepreneurs must be able to effectively network and build relationships in order to secure funding, build a team, and grow their business. They are often skilled at connecting with others and building mutually beneficial relationships.
- Financial acumen: Entrepreneurs must have a good understanding of finance and

be able to manage their finances effectively. This includes creating and sticking to a budget, managing cash flow, and understanding financial statements.

- Leadership: Entrepreneurs must be able to effectively lead and manage their team in order to achieve their goals. They must be able to inspire and motivate their team to work towards a common goal.

While not all entrepreneurs possess all of these characteristics, they are often a combination of several of these traits that enable them to succeed in their business ventures.

Benefits of Being an Entrepreneur

Being an entrepreneur can bring a wide range of benefits, both personal and professional. Here are some of the key benefits of entrepreneurship:

- Financial Independence: Entrepreneurs have the potential to earn a significant income and control their financial future. They have the opportunity to create wealth and achieve financial stability through the success of their business.
- Freedom and Flexibility: Entrepreneurs have the freedom to set their own schedules and work on their own terms. They have the flexibility to work from anywhere, whether that's from home or on the go, and have the ability to balance their work and personal life as they see fit.
- Job Satisfaction: Entrepreneurs have the ability to turn their passion into a career and build a business that aligns with their values and interests. This leads to a high level of job satisfaction, as they are able to spend their days doing something they love.
- Creative Control: Entrepreneurs have the ability to make decisions and bring their ideas to life without having to answer to a boss or board of directors. They have complete creative control over their business and can bring their unique vision to life.
- Personal Growth: Starting a business requires entrepreneurs to wear many hats and take on a wide range of responsibilities. This leads to personal growth and development, as they learn new skills and gain experience in areas they may not have previously considered.
- Making a Difference: Entrepreneurs have the ability to make a positive impact on their communities and the world. Whether through creating jobs, developing innovative products, or giving back to their communities, entrepreneurs have the power to make a difference and leave a lasting legacy.

In summary, being an entrepreneur offers a unique set of benefits that can bring financial independence, freedom, job satisfaction, creative control, personal growth, and the ability to make a positive impact.

Pivoting and making key decisions

Pivoting and making key decisions are critical components of entrepreneurship. Every business faces challenges and obstacles, and it's essential for entrepreneurs to have the flexibility and resilience to navigate these challenges and make decisions that will move their business forward. In this part, we'll explore the concept of pivoting, why it's important, and how to make key decisions that will help you succeed as an entrepreneur.

Pivoting refers to the process of changing direction in response to market conditions or changes in your business environment. It's the act of adapting your business strategy to align with new realities, opportunities, or challenges. Pivoting is essential for entrepreneurs because it allows them to remain agile and responsive to changes in their market and environment. When done effectively, pivoting can help entrepreneurs stay ahead of the curve and capitalize on new opportunities.

Making key decisions is another critical component of entrepreneurship. Entrepreneurs must be able to make sound decisions based on their goals, values, and the best interests of their business. Key decisions can range from decisions about product development and marketing strategies to decisions about funding, hiring, and organizational structure. Entrepreneurs must be able to assess their options and make informed decisions that will drive their business forward.

One of the most important things to keep in mind when pivoting and making key decisions is to stay true to your core values and mission. Your values and mission should guide your decision-making and inform your pivoting strategy. Additionally, it's essential to stay focused on your long-term goals and vision, even as you navigate short-term challenges and obstacles.

To make effective pivots and key decisions, entrepreneurs must also be willing to take calculated risks. Entrepreneurship is inherently risky, and you'll need to be comfortable with uncertainty and risk-taking if you want to succeed. However, it's important to remember that not all risks are created equal, and you'll need to carefully evaluate the risks and benefits of each decision you make.

Finally, it's essential to stay informed and keep up with industry trends and changes. Staying informed will help you identify new opportunities, anticipate challenges, and make informed decisions that will help you succeed.

In conclusion, pivoting and making key decisions are critical components of entrepreneurship. Entrepreneurs must be able to adapt to changes in their market and environment, make sound decisions based on their goals, values, and the best interests of their business, and take calculated risks to drive their business forward. By staying true to your core values, focusing on your long-term goals, and staying informed about industry trends, you can make the pivots and key decisions that will help you fuel your dreams and succeed as an entrepreneur.

The Art of pivoting

Pivoting is a critical component of successful entrepreneurship and business growth, but it can also be challenging. Making a change in direction can be difficult for a company, especially if it has been following a particular strategy for some time. However, being able to pivot effectively can mean the difference between a company that thrives and one that fails.

One important factor in successful pivoting is to be open to new ideas and approaches. This means that entrepreneurs and business owners must be willing to question their assumptions and be receptive to feedback and suggestions from their employees, customers, and other stakeholders. By staying open-minded and being willing to learn and grow, companies can stay ahead of the curve and be better prepared to navigate challenges and changes in the market.

Another important factor is to have a clear understanding of the company's core strengths and value proposition. When a business is faced with a change in market conditions or other challenges, it's important to focus on what makes it unique and valuable to its customers. By leveraging these strengths, companies can differentiate themselves from their competitors and remain competitive even as the market evolves.

Finally, businesses must be prepared to move quickly and decisively when the time comes to pivot. This means having the right processes and systems in place to support rapid decision-making and execution, as well as the ability to adapt and change course as needed. By being nimble and responsive, companies can stay ahead of the curve and remain competitive in a rapidly changing business landscape.

In conclusion, pivoting is an important skill for entrepreneurs and business owners, and requires a combination of strategic thinking, open-mindedness, focus on core strengths, and a willingness to take decisive action. By mastering the art of pivoting, businesses can position themselves for long-term success and thrive in an ever-changing marketplace.

Entrepreneurial Mindset and habits

Entrepreneurial Mindset and Habits refer to the attitudes, beliefs, and behaviors that successful entrepreneurs possess and cultivate.

For example, an entrepreneurial mindset emphasizes risk-taking, creativity, and a willingness to learn and grow. Entrepreneurs who cultivate this mindset are better equipped to overcome obstacles and see challenges as opportunities for growth. Habits such as goal-setting, self-discipline, and effective time management can also contribute to the success of an entrepreneur by helping them prioritize their goals and stay focused on achieving them.

By developing a growth mindset and continuously seeking new knowledge and skills, entrepreneurs can stay ahead of the curve and stay competitive in their respective fields. Additionally, this section could touch on the importance of self-reflection and introspection for entrepreneurs, as it allows them to continually assess their habits, mindset, and behaviors to identify areas for improvement.

Overall, the Entrepreneurial Mindset and Habits section aims to emphasize the importance of developing a positive and proactive attitude and set of behaviors for entrepreneurs to achieve their goals and succeed in their ventures.

Having an entrepreneurial mindset and cultivating the right habits can make all the difference in achieving success as an entrepreneur. It's important for entrepreneurs to have a positive and proactive attitude, as well as the ability to take calculated risks. Entrepreneurs who are creative and willing to learn and grow are more likely to overcome obstacles and see challenges as opportunities for growth.

Goal-setting is also a key habit for entrepreneurs. By setting clear and achievable goals, entrepreneurs can stay focused and motivated. Self-discipline is also critical, as it allows entrepreneurs to prioritize their time and energy towards their most important tasks.

Effective time management is essential, as entrepreneurs often wear many hats and must balance multiple responsibilities.

Continuous learning and personal development are also crucial for entrepreneurs. By developing a growth mindset and continuously seeking new knowledge and skills, entrepreneurs can stay ahead of the curve and stay competitive in their respective fields. This can be achieved through reading, attending seminars and workshops, or working with a mentor.

Self-reflection and introspection are also important for entrepreneurs, as it allows them to assess their habits, mindset, and behaviors to identify areas for improvement. This can be done through journaling, meditation, or seeking feedback from others. By being self-aware and continually working on themselves, entrepreneurs can make adjustments and improvements to their habits and mindset to achieve their goals more effectively.

In conclusion, the entrepreneurial mindset and habits play a crucial role in the success of an entrepreneur. By developing a positive and proactive attitude, cultivating the right habits, and continually learning and growing, entrepreneurs can set themselves up for success and achieve their goals.

Identifying and Validating Your Business Idea

The benefits of being an entrepreneur are many and can include financial independence, the ability to bring your vision to life, and the freedom to be your own boss. However, becoming an entrepreneur is not without its challenges, and it's important to thoroughly assess and validate your business idea before taking the leap.

Identifying and validating your business idea involves conducting market research to assess the demand for your product or service and determining if there is a viable market for it. This can involve conducting surveys, talking to potential customers, and analyzing data on your target market. The goal is to get a clear understanding of the needs and wants of your target market, as well as any existing competition, in order to determine if your idea is worth pursuing.

One key component of validating your business idea is conducting a feasibility study, which is an in-depth analysis of the viability of your business idea. This can include a detailed examination of your target market, competition, and financial projections. The goal is to determine if your idea is realistic and has a good chance of succeeding in the market.

It's also important to assess your own skills and abilities, as well as the resources you have available, in order to determine if you have what it takes to bring your idea to life. This can include assessing your own entrepreneurial skills, as well as your financial resources and support network.

In conclusion, taking the time to thoroughly validate your business idea before launching can help you avoid costly mistakes and increase your chances of success. By conducting market research, conducting a feasibility study, and assessing your own skills and resources, you can gain a clear understanding of the viability of your idea and make an informed decision on whether or not to pursue it.

Conducting Market Research

Conducting market research is an important aspect of the process of starting a new business. The goal is to gather information about your target market, competition, and potential challenges to help you make informed decisions and increase your chances of success.

Defining your target market:
One of the first steps in conducting market research is defining your target market. This involves identifying the specific group of people who are most likely to buy your product or service, taking into account factors such as age, gender, income, and location, among others.

Gathering data:
Once you have defined your target market, the next step is to gather data. This can be done through various methods such as surveys, analyzing existing data, and talking to potential customers. The goal is to gather as much information as possible about your target market, including their needs, wants, and buying habits.

Analyzing the competition:
In addition to gathering information about your target market, it is important to analyze the competition. This involves researching your competitors and understanding their strengths and weaknesses, including their products or services, marketing strategies, and pricing.

Assessing demand:

Assessing demand is another important aspect of market research. This involves determining the potential demand for your product or service and how it fits into the larger market. This can be done through surveys, analyzing sales data, and talking to industry experts.

Evaluating potential risks and challenges:

Finally, it's important to evaluate potential risks and challenges associated with your business idea. This includes identifying potential challenges and risks such as competition, changing market conditions, and technological advancements.

Conducting market research can also involve using tools and techniques such as focus groups, consumer panels, and data analytics. The goal is to gather as much information as possible to help inform your decisions and increase your chances of success.

It's important to keep in mind that market research is an ongoing process and should be conducted regularly to stay up-to-date on changes in the market and customer needs. By conducting thorough market research, you can gain a better understanding of your target market and competition, and make informed decisions about how to bring your business idea to life.

In conclusion, conducting market research is an essential step in the process of launching a new business. By gathering information about your target market, competition, and potential risks, you can make informed decisions about how to bring your idea to life and increase your chances of success.

Identifying Your Target Market

Identifying your target market is a critical step in the process of launching a new business. It involves defining the specific group of people who are most likely to buy your product or service, and understanding their needs, wants, and buying habits. This information is crucial for making informed decisions about your marketing, pricing, and product development strategies.

There are several key components to identifying your target market, including:

Demographic information is one of the key components of identifying your target market as it helps you understand who your potential customers are and what their purchasing habits might be. Factors such as age, gender, income, education level, and location can all influence a person's purchasing decisions and can help you determine the best marketing strategies for your target market.

Psychographic information involves understanding your target market's values, interests, and lifestyle choices. By understanding what motivates your potential customers and what they are looking for in a product or service, you can better tailor your marketing efforts to reach them.

Knowing your target market's buying habits is also important as it helps you determine the best way to reach them and what marketing strategies will be most effective. Understanding when and where your target market makes purchasing decisions can help you develop a sales strategy that targets them at the right time and in the right place.

Analyzing your competition and understanding their target market is also important as it helps you differentiate yourself from them and better serve your target market. By gathering customer feedback, you can gain insight into your target market's preferences and make informed decisions about product development and marketing strategies.

It's important to keep in mind that your target market may change over time as your business grows and evolves. By continuously gathering information about your target market and making informed decisions about your marketing and product development strategies, you can ensure that your business remains relevant and continues to grow.

In conclusion, identifying your target market is a critical step in the process of launching a new business. By understanding the needs, wants, and buying habits of your potential customers, you can make informed decisions about your marketing, pricing, and product development strategies and increase your chances of success.

Evaluating the Feasibility of Your Business Idea

Evaluating the feasibility of your business idea is an important step in the process of launching a new venture. It involves examining the potential for success of your idea, and determining whether it is viable in the current market. By conducting a thorough feasibility analysis, you can make informed decisions about whether to move forward with your idea, and if so, how to best bring it to life.

There are several key components to evaluating the feasibility of your business idea, including:

- Market research: Market research involves gathering information about your target market and competition, and evaluating the potential demand for your product or service. This information can help you determine whether your business idea is viable and whether there is a market for it. Market research typically includes identifying your target customers, understanding their needs and preferences, and analyzing your competition. This information can help you make informed decisions about your product, pricing, marketing strategies, and overall business strategy.
- Financial analysis: Financial analysis involves evaluating the costs associated with launching and operating your business, as well as assessing your financial resources to bring the idea to life. This may include analyzing potential profits and losses, conducting a break-even analysis, and determining the amount of funding you need to start and run your business. A thorough financial analysis can help you identify potential risks and challenges, as well as opportunities for growth and profitability.
- Legal and regulatory considerations: Legal and regulatory considerations involve researching and understanding the laws and regulations that apply to

your business. This may include identifying any licenses or permits required to operate your business, complying with tax laws, and protecting your intellectual property. Failing to comply with legal and regulatory requirements can result in legal penalties and other consequences, so it is important to ensure that you are in compliance before launching your business.

- Technical feasibility: Technical feasibility involves evaluating the technology required to bring your business idea to life, as well as assessing the skills and expertise of your team. This may include assessing whether you have the technical knowledge and resources required to build and maintain the necessary systems and infrastructure, such as a website, software, or hardware. Ensuring technical feasibility is critical to ensuring that your business can operate effectively and meet the needs of your customers.

- Operational feasibility: Operational feasibility involves evaluating the operational processes and systems required to run your business effectively, as well as assessing the capabilities of your team to manage these processes. This may include assessing your team's skills and experience, identifying potential operational challenges, and developing strategies to mitigate these challenges. Ensuring operational feasibility is critical to ensuring that your business can operate effectively and efficiently, and that you can deliver a high-quality product or service to your customers.

In conclusion, evaluating the feasibility of your business idea is an important step in the process of launching a new venture. By conducting a thorough analysis of the potential for success, you can make informed decisions about whether to move forward with your idea, and if so, how to best bring it to life.

Developing a Business Plan

Developing a Business Plan is a critical step in the process of starting a new business or launching a new product or service. A well-crafted business plan not only helps entrepreneurs clarify their goals and strategies, but it also serves as a roadmap for their business and can help them secure funding and investment.

The business plan should include a detailed description of the business, including the products or services offered, target market, competition, and financial projections. Understanding the importance of a business plan is the first step in the process of developing one. A business plan serves as a reference point for entrepreneurs as they build their business, and it helps them stay focused on their goals and objectives.

The key components of a business plan typically include an executive summary, market analysis, organization and management structure, product or service offerings, marketing and sales strategies, and financial projections. The executive summary should provide a high-level overview of the business, including its mission, vision, and key objectives. The market analysis should detail the size and growth potential of the target market and the competition in the industry.

The organization and management structure should describe the roles and responsibilities of key personnel, as well as the ownership structure of the business. The product or service offerings section should detail the features and benefits of the products or services offered and how they meet the needs of the target market.

The marketing and sales strategies should outline the methods used to reach the target market, such as advertising, public relations, and direct marketing. The financial projections should include detailed projections of revenue, expenses, and profits for a minimum of three to five years.

In conclusion, developing a comprehensive business plan is a vital step in the process of starting and growing a successful business. It serves as a roadmap for entrepreneurs and helps them secure funding, attract and retain employees, and achieve their goals and objectives.

Understanding the Importance of a Business Plan

A business plan is a comprehensive document that outlines the goals and objectives of a business, and the strategies and tactics for achieving them. It is a roadmap for success, and a key tool for securing investment and financing, as well as for guiding the growth and development of a business over time. Understanding the importance of a business plan is crucial for any entrepreneur who is serious about success.

There are several key benefits to having a well-crafted business plan, including:
- Clarity of vision and purpose: A business plan provides a clear and concise articulation of a business's goals and objectives, and the strategies for achieving them. This clarity of vision and purpose can help guide the growth and development of a business, and ensure that all stakeholders are aligned and working towards the same goals.
- Better decision-making: A business plan provides a roadmap for success, and helps entrepreneurs make informed decisions about their business. It helps entrepreneurs think through all of the key components of their business, including the target market, competition, marketing and sales strategies, and financial projections, and provides a framework for making informed decisions.
- Attracting investment and financing: A well-crafted business plan is often a critical component of securing investment and financing for a business. Investors and lenders use business plans to evaluate the potential for success of a business, and to determine whether they should invest or lend money to the business.
- Facilitating growth and development: A business plan provides a roadmap for growth and development, and helps entrepreneurs stay focused and on track. It helps entrepreneurs think through all of the key components of their business, including their target market, competition, marketing and sales strategies, and

financial projections, and provides a framework for making informed decisions about growth and development.

- Measuring progress and success: A business plan provides a benchmark for measuring progress and success, and helps entrepreneurs determine whether they are on track to meet their goals and objectives. It provides a framework for tracking progress, and for making informed decisions about changes and adjustments that may be required to ensure success.

In conclusion, understanding the importance of a business plan is crucial for any entrepreneur who is serious about success. A well-crafted business plan provides a clear and concise articulation of a business's goals and objectives, and the strategies and tactics for achieving them. It is a key tool for securing investment and financing, as well as for guiding the growth and development of a business over time.

Key Components of a Business Plan

A business plan is a comprehensive document that outlines the goals and objectives of a business, and the strategies and tactics for achieving them. It serves as a roadmap for success, and is essential for securing investment and financing, as well as for guiding the growth and development of a business over time. There are several key components of a business plan, which are essential for its effectiveness.

Executive Summary:
- The executive summary is often the first and most important section of a business plan, as it sets the tone for the rest of the document. It should be written in a clear, concise, and compelling manner, and should include the most important information about the business, such as its goals and objectives, target market, competitive landscape, and financial projections. The executive summary should be tailored to the audience and should highlight the most important points of the business plan.

Business Description:
- The business description provides a more detailed overview of the business, including its history, mission statement, products or services, management team, and legal structure. It should provide a clear and concise picture of the business, and should highlight its unique strengths and capabilities. The business description should also explain how the business will generate revenue and create value for its customers.

Market Analysis:
- The market analysis section provides a thorough analysis of the target market, including demographic information, buying habits, and customer needs and preferences. It should also provide a detailed assessment of the competition,

including their strengths and weaknesses, and a discussion of the opportunities and challenges facing the business. The market analysis should be based on sound research and should provide a comprehensive understanding of the market and its dynamics.

Marketing and Sales Strategies:

- The marketing and sales strategies section outlines the strategies and tactics for reaching and selling to the target market. It should include information on product positioning, pricing, promotion, and distribution, as well as a detailed plan for developing and maintaining relationships with customers and partners. The marketing and sales strategies should be aligned with the overall goals and objectives of the business and should be based on a sound understanding of the market and its needs.

Financial Projections:

- The financial projections section provides a detailed financial analysis of the business, including revenue and expense projections, cash flow analysis, and a balance sheet. It should also provide a comprehensive analysis of the key drivers of the business, including sales, costs, and profitability. The financial projections should be based on sound assumptions and should provide a realistic assessment of the financial performance of the business over time.

Appendices and Supporting Documents:

- The appendices and supporting documents section includes any additional information that is relevant to the business plan, including resumes of key personnel, contracts, licenses, and permits. This section should provide supporting evidence for the claims and projections made in the other sections of the business plan. The appendices and supporting documents should be well-organized and should be easily accessible to the reader.

In summary, a well-crafted business plan should include all of these key components and should be tailored to the specific needs of the business and its target audience. The business plan should be based on sound research, analysis, and financial projections, and should provide a clear and compelling vision of the business and its potential for success.

Setting Realistic Goals and Objectives

Setting realistic goals and objectives is an important aspect of developing a successful business plan. Goals and objectives serve as a roadmap for entrepreneurs, helping them focus their efforts and resources towards the most important aspects of their business. By setting realistic goals and objectives, entrepreneurs can measure their progress and make necessary adjustments along the way to ensure they are on track towards success.

When setting goals and objectives, it is important to be specific and measurable. Rather than setting broad, general goals like "grow the business," entrepreneurs should set specific and measurable goals like "increase sales by 20% within the next year." This type of goal is more concrete and easier to track progress towards.

It is also important to set both short-term and long-term goals. Short-term goals should be achievable within the next year and help entrepreneurs build momentum towards their long-term goals. Long-term goals should be more ambitious and provide a vision for the future of the business.

In addition to setting specific and measurable goals, it is also important to prioritize them. Entrepreneurs should focus on the most important goals first and allocate resources accordingly. This helps them stay focused on what is most important and avoid becoming sidetracked by less important goals.

Finally, it is important to review and adjust goals and objectives regularly. Entrepreneurs should regularly assess their progress towards their goals and make adjustments as needed. This helps them stay on track and make course corrections as necessary.

In conclusion, setting realistic goals and objectives is a critical aspect of developing a successful business plan. By being specific, measurable, prioritized, and regularly reviewed, goals and objectives provide a roadmap for entrepreneurs and help them stay focused on what is most important as they build and grow their business.

Securing Funding and Investment

Securing funding and investment is a crucial step for many entrepreneurs in the early stages of their business. Whether it is to cover startup costs, fund growth initiatives, or bring on key personnel, having access to capital is essential for businesses to succeed.

When it comes to securing funding and investment, entrepreneurs have several options to consider, including traditional lending sources, grants, angel investors, venture capital firms, and crowdfunding. Each option has its own pros and cons, and entrepreneurs should carefully evaluate their options and choose the one that best fits their needs.

To secure funding and investment, entrepreneurs need to be prepared to make a pitch to potential investors. This typically involves creating a pitch deck that showcases the business idea, target market, financial projections, and the value proposition. Entrepreneurs should focus on demonstrating why their business is a good investment opportunity and how they plan to use the funds to grow and scale their business.

Networking with potential investors is also an important part of securing funding and investment. Entrepreneurs should attend events, meet with venture capitalists and angel investors, and build relationships with members of their industry. By establishing a network of investors and advisors, entrepreneurs can increase their chances of securing funding and investment and gain valuable insights and advice along the way.

In conclusion, securing funding and investment is a critical aspect of starting and growing a successful business. Entrepreneurs need to carefully evaluate their options, be prepared to pitch their business, and network with potential investors in order to secure the funding they need to succeed.

Understanding Your Funding Options

One of the most important decisions that entrepreneurs face when starting a business is how to secure funding. There are several options available, each with its own advantages and disadvantages, and it is important to understand the different options and choose the one that is best suited to the needs of the business.

Bootstrapping:
This is a way to start and grow a business using personal savings and revenue generated by the business, without taking on any external investment or debt. It can be a low-risk option, as it doesn't involve giving up equity in the business or incurring debt. However, it can be difficult to scale the business quickly without access to additional funds.

Crowdfunding:
Crowdfunding involves raising funds from a large number of people, usually via the internet, in exchange for rewards or equity in the business. This can be a great option for businesses that have a compelling product or idea, and a large and engaged online community. However, it can be difficult to secure significant funding through crowdfunding, and the funds raised may not be enough to fully fund the business.

Angel Investment:
Angel investment involves receiving investment from high net worth individuals who are willing to invest in early-stage businesses in exchange for equity. Angel investors can provide not only funding, but also mentorship, networks, and other resources that can help the business grow and succeed. However, angel investors can also be demanding and may want a significant amount of control over the business.

Venture Capital:
Venture capital involves receiving investment from venture capital firms, which specialize in investing in high-potential startups in exchange for equity. Venture capital firms can provide significant amounts of funding, as well as expertise and networks, to help the business grow and succeed. However, venture capital firms can also be demanding and may require a significant amount of control over the business.

Bank Loans:
Bank loans involve borrowing funds from a bank or other financial institution, in exchange for a loan repayment agreement and interest payments. Bank loans can provide a significant amount of funding, but they can also be difficult to secure and may require collateral or a personal guarantee.

In summary, bootstrapping is a low-risk option for starting and growing a business, but it may limit the ability to scale quickly. Crowdfunding can be a good option for businesses with a compelling product or idea, but it may not provide enough funding. Angel investment and venture capital can both provide significant funding and resources, but may come with demands and requirements from investors. Bank loans can provide significant funding, but can be difficult to secure and may come with high interest rates or collateral requirements.

In conclusion, understanding your funding options is an important step in securing the funding that is needed to start and grow a successful business. Entrepreneurs should consider the advantages and disadvantages of each option, and choose the one that is best suited to their needs and goals. A well-crafted business plan, along with a clear understanding of the target market, the competition, and the goals and objectives of the business, can help to increase the chances of securing the funding that is needed to succeed.

Preparing a Pitch Deck

A pitch deck is a visual presentation that provides an overview of a business, its products or services, and its plans for growth and success. It is typically used to convince potential investors, partners, or customers to support the business, either through investment, collaboration, or purchase. A well-prepared pitch deck can be a powerful tool for convincing others to support your business, and can help to secure the funding, resources, and partners that are needed to grow and succeed.

Here are some key components of a effective pitch deck:
- Introduction: Start by introducing the problem that your business is solving, and explaining why it is important. Provide a brief overview of your business, its products or services, and its target market.
- Market Opportunity: Describe the market opportunity for your business, including the size of the market, the growth potential, and the competitive landscape. Highlight any unique features or benefits of your product or service, and explain why it is better than existing solutions.
- Business Model: Explain how your business makes money, including any revenue streams and pricing strategies. Provide an overview of your costs and margins, and explain how you will scale the business over time.
- Team: Introduce the key members of your team, including their backgrounds, skills, and experience. Explain why they are well-suited to succeed with this business, and highlight any relevant successes or accomplishments.
- Traction: Provide evidence of the progress that the business has made so far, including any early adopters, customers, or partnerships. Explain why this is an indicator of future success, and highlight any metrics that demonstrate the potential of the business.

- Financial Projections: Provide financial projections for the business, including revenue, costs, margins, and cash flow. Explain how you arrived at these projections, and highlight any key assumptions or risks.
- Ask: End the pitch by making a clear and compelling ask, such as seeking investment, a partnership, or a customer. Explain why the business is a good opportunity for the audience, and how they can get involved.

In conclusion, a pitch deck is a critical tool for convincing others to support your business, and can help to secure the funding, resources, and partners that are needed to grow and succeed. A well-prepared pitch deck should be clear, concise, and compelling, and should effectively communicate the key components of your business, including the market opportunity, the business model, the team, the traction, and the financial projections. Additionally, it should make a clear and compelling ask, and explain why the business is a good opportunity for the audience.

Networking with Investors

Networking with investors is an important aspect of securing funding and investment for entrepreneurs. By establishing relationships with potential investors, entrepreneurs can increase their chances of securing funding and gain valuable insights and advice along the way.

Networking with investors can take many forms, including attending events and conferences, reaching out to venture capitalists and angel investors, and building relationships with members of their industry. Entrepreneurs should seek out opportunities to connect with potential investors and start building relationships long before they need funding. This can help them to establish trust and credibility with potential investors and increase their chances of securing funding when the time comes.

When networking with investors, entrepreneurs should be prepared to discuss their business idea and value proposition. They should also be open to feedback and be willing to listen to potential investors' perspectives and advice. Entrepreneurs should also be prepared to discuss their financial projections and demonstrate how they plan to use the funds they receive to grow and scale their business.

In conclusion, networking with investors is an important aspect of securing funding and investment for entrepreneurs. By establishing relationships with potential investors, entrepreneurs can increase their chances of securing funding and gain valuable insights and advice along the way. Entrepreneurs should seek out opportunities to connect with potential investors, be prepared to discuss their business idea, and be open to feedback and advice.

Networking with Investors
Networking is a critical component of securing investment for your business. Investors are more likely to invest in businesses that they know, like, and trust, and building strong

relationships with them can be the key to securing the funding that you need to grow and succeed. Here are some tips for networking with investors:

- Attend events: Attend industry events, conferences, and networking events where investors are likely to be present. These events provide an opportunity to meet investors, learn about their interests and investment criteria, and make a positive impression.
- Leverage your network: Ask your friends, family, and colleagues if they know any investors, and if they can make an introduction. Your existing network can be a valuable resource for connecting with potential investors.
- Utilize online networks: Join online networks, such as LinkedIn and AngelList, where you can connect with investors and learn about investment opportunities.
- Be prepared: When you meet with investors, be prepared to present your business, its products or services, and its plans for growth and success. Have a clear and concise pitch, and be able to answer any questions that they may have.
- Follow up: After you meet with investors, follow up with them to stay in touch and continue building the relationship. This can include sending them updates about your business, inviting them to events, and asking for their advice and feedback.

Crowdfunding and Alternative Funding Sources

Crowdfunding is a type of funding that allows entrepreneurs to raise money from a large number of people, usually via the internet. There are different types of crowdfunding, including reward-based crowdfunding, where individuals contribute money in exchange for a reward, such as a product or service, and equity-based crowdfunding, where investors contribute money in exchange for a small ownership stake in the business. Crowdfunding can be a good option for entrepreneurs who have a compelling idea or product and a large and engaged online community. However, it can be challenging to secure significant funding through crowdfunding, and the funds raised may not be enough to fully fund the business.

Alternative funding sources include venture capital, angel investment, and microfinance. Venture capital firms invest in high-potential startups in exchange for equity, providing not only funding, but also expertise and networks to help the business grow and succeed. Angel investors are typically high net worth individuals who invest in early-stage businesses in exchange for equity, and can provide funding, mentorship, networks, and other resources. Microfinance involves providing small loans to entrepreneurs, often in developing countries, to help them start or grow their businesses. Each of these funding sources has its benefits and drawbacks, and entrepreneurs must carefully consider which option is best for their business.

It's also important to note the role of government grants and loans in supporting entrepreneurship. These funding options can provide entrepreneurs with access to low-interest loans, tax incentives, and other financial support to help them start and grow their businesses. However, entrepreneurs must understand the criteria and requirements for securing these types of funding and ensure they meet all eligibility criteria before applying.

Additionally, online lending platforms such as peer-to-peer (P2P) lending can be a viable alternative funding source, allowing entrepreneurs to connect with individual investors who are interested in funding their businesses. Equity crowdfunding is another alternative funding source that enables entrepreneurs to raise capital from a large number of individual investors in exchange for a small share of ownership in their business.

Overall, it's important for entrepreneurs to thoroughly research and understand the terms and conditions of each funding source and to carefully consider the impact on their business and personal financial situation before making a decision. By exploring and utilizing various funding sources, entrepreneurs can increase their chances of securing the capital they need to achieve their business goals.

It is also important for entrepreneurs to create a strong financial plan and to regularly review their financial position to ensure they are on track to achieving their business goals.

By carefully exploring and utilizing various funding sources, entrepreneurs can secure the capital they need to fuel their dreams and take their businesses to the next level.

Building a Strong Team

Building a strong team is an essential component of entrepreneurial success. The right team can help an entrepreneur achieve their goals, bring new perspectives and ideas to the table, and provide the support and resources needed to grow and scale the business.

When building a team, entrepreneurs should start by defining the roles and responsibilities of each team member. This will help to ensure that everyone is on the same page and working towards the same goals. Entrepreneurs should also look for team members who complement their own skills and strengths and who share their passion for the business.

In addition to defining roles and responsibilities, entrepreneurs should also focus on creating a positive and collaborative work environment. This can be achieved through clear communication, regular feedback, and a focus on personal and professional growth for each team member. Entrepreneurs should also be open to new ideas and perspectives and encourage their team to take an active role in decision-making.

Hiring and managing employees is also an important aspect of building a strong team. Entrepreneurs should take the time to carefully evaluate potential employees and ensure that they are a good fit for the company culture and the business goals. They should also invest in training and development opportunities for their employees to help them grow and succeed in their roles.

In conclusion, building a strong team is an essential component of entrepreneurial success. Entrepreneurs should define roles and responsibilities, focus on creating a positive and collaborative work environment, and invest in hiring and managing employees. By building a strong team, entrepreneurs can achieve their goals, bring new perspectives and ideas to the table, and provide the support and resources needed to grow and scale their business.

Importance of Building a Strong Team

The Importance of Building a Strong Team

Having a strong and dedicated team is one of the key factors in the success of any business. A team that works well together, is motivated and engaged, and has a clear understanding of its goals and objectives, can help to drive the growth and success of a business, and overcome any obstacles that may arise. Here are some of the reasons why building a strong team is so important:

- Improved productivity: A strong team is more productive than a group of individuals working alone. Teams can pool their resources, skills, and expertise to tackle tasks more efficiently, and can provide each other with support and motivation to help them achieve their goals.
- Enhanced creativity: Teams bring together diverse perspectives and ideas, and can encourage innovation and creativity. This can lead to new and better solutions to problems, and help to keep the business competitive and ahead of the curve.
- Increased motivation: Teams provide a sense of belonging and community, which can help to increase the motivation and engagement of each team member. This, in turn, can lead to better performance, increased job satisfaction, and a stronger commitment to the success of the business.
- Shared responsibility: Teams share the responsibility for the success of a project or task, which can help to distribute the workload, reduce stress, and increase accountability. This can lead to better results, and a stronger sense of shared ownership and responsibility for the success of the business.
- Better decision-making: Teams can make better decisions than individuals working alone, as they bring together diverse perspectives and can consider a wider range of options and consequences. This can lead to more informed and effective decision-making, and help to ensure the success of the business.

In conclusion, building a strong team is essential for the success of any business. By bringing together a diverse group of individuals with different skills, perspectives, and ideas, you can create a team that is more productive, creative, motivated, and effective than any individual working alone. By focusing on building a strong and dedicated team, you can help to drive the growth and success of your business, and overcome any challenges that may arise.

Hiring and Managing Employees

Hiring and managing employees is one of the most important and challenging tasks that any business owner or manager faces. To be successful, it is important to understand the key components of an effective hiring and management process, and to develop the skills and strategies needed to attract, retain, and motivate employees.

Here are some key tips and considerations to help you succeed:
- Define your hiring needs: Before you start the hiring process, it is important to determine what specific skills, experience, and qualities you are looking for in a candidate. This will help you to focus your search and ensure that you are attracting the right candidates for your business.
- Develop a strong job description: A well-written job description can help you to attract the right candidates, and to clearly communicate your expectations and requirements. Be sure to include information about the job duties, qualifications, and any specific skills or experience that are required.
- Use a comprehensive hiring process: A comprehensive hiring process should include an application and resume review, interviews, reference checks, and any other assessments or evaluations that are needed to determine a candidate's fit for your business. Be sure to be consistent in your hiring process, and to treat all candidates fairly and equally.
- Onboard new hires effectively: Onboarding is an important part of the hiring process, and can help to set the tone for your new employee's success. Be sure to provide new hires with the training, resources, and support that they need to succeed, and to help them to quickly become integrated into your team.
- Foster a positive work environment: A positive work environment is essential for attracting and retaining employees, and can help to improve motivation

and job satisfaction. Be sure to communicate clearly, provide opportunities for professional development, and create an environment that is respectful, supportive, and inclusive.

- Manage performance effectively: Effective performance management is critical for ensuring that your employees are meeting your expectations, and for helping them to develop and improve their skills. Be sure to set clear performance expectations, provide regular feedback, and recognize and reward good performance.
- Invest in employee development: Investing in the development and growth of your employees can help to improve their skills, increase their motivation, and reduce turnover. Be sure to provide opportunities for professional development, such as training, mentorship, and coaching, and to support your employees in their career growth.

In conclusion, hiring and managing employees is a critical component of any successful business. By following these tips and considerations, you can create a strong and dedicated team that is motivated, productive, and committed to the success of your business. By investing in your employees and creating a positive work environment, you can help to attract and retain the best talent, and drive the growth and success of your business.

Building a Culture of Collaboration and Innovation

Building a culture of collaboration and innovation is crucial for entrepreneurial success. A strong culture can foster creativity, encourage teamwork, and promote a sense of purpose and belonging among employees.

To build a culture of collaboration and innovation, entrepreneurs should start by setting a positive tone and promoting open communication. Encouraging team members to share their ideas and opinions can help to create a supportive environment where new ideas can be developed and refined. Entrepreneurs should also encourage their team to take risks and think outside the box, and recognize and reward those who come up with innovative solutions.

In addition to promoting open communication, entrepreneurs should also invest in training and development opportunities for their employees. This can include workshops, conferences, and other opportunities for learning and growth. By investing in their employees, entrepreneurs can help them to develop the skills and knowledge they need to be successful and innovative in their roles.

Another important aspect of building a culture of collaboration and innovation is encouraging team members to work together on projects and initiatives. Collaboration can lead to new and innovative solutions, and can help to foster a sense of teamwork and camaraderie among team members.

In conclusion, building a culture of collaboration and innovation is essential for entrepreneurial success. Entrepreneurs should promote open communication, invest in employee training and development, and encourage team members to work together on projects and initiatives. By building a strong culture, entrepreneurs can foster creativity, encourage teamwork, and promote a sense of purpose and belonging among employees.

Building a Culture of Collaboration and Innovation
- Creating a culture of collaboration and innovation is critical for the success of

any business. By fostering a collaborative and innovative environment, you can drive new ideas, improve processes, and increase productivity, creativity, and overall success. Here are some key tips and considerations for building a culture of collaboration and innovation in your business:

- Encourage open communication: Encouraging open communication is essential for fostering collaboration and innovation. Encourage employees to share their ideas, opinions, and feedback, and to work together to identify solutions to problems and challenges.
- Promote a culture of experimentation: A culture of experimentation is critical for fostering innovation. Encourage employees to test new ideas and approaches, and to take calculated risks. This can help to drive new thinking, new solutions, and increased innovation.
- Foster a sense of ownership and accountability: A sense of ownership and accountability is important for encouraging collaboration and innovation. Encourage employees to take responsibility for their work and their contributions, and to feel empowered to make decisions and take action.
- Provide opportunities for cross-functional collaboration: Cross-functional collaboration is an important part of fostering collaboration and innovation. Encourage employees from different departments, functions, and areas of expertise to work together, share ideas, and explore new solutions.
- Recognize and reward collaboration and innovation: Recognizing and rewarding collaboration and innovation can help to drive engagement, motivation, and creativity. Be sure to recognize and reward employees for their contributions, ideas, and innovations, and to celebrate successes and achievements.
- Lead by example: Leading by example is critical for building a culture of collaboration and innovation. As a leader, you can model the behaviors, attitudes, and values that you want to see in your team, and encourage others to follow your lead.

In conclusion, building a culture of collaboration and innovation is essential for the success of any business. By encouraging open communication, promoting a culture of experimentation, fostering a sense of ownership and accountability, providing opportunities for cross-functional collaboration, recognizing and rewarding collaboration and innovation, and leading by example, you can drive new ideas, improve processes, and increase productivity, creativity, and overall success.

Building a Diverse and Inclusive Business: Strategies for Entrepreneurs

Diversity and inclusion are essential components of any successful business in today's world. They are not only moral and ethical values, but they also improve creativity, innovation, and overall performance. A diverse and inclusive work environment promotes employee engagement, reduces turnover, and attracts talent from different backgrounds. In this section, we will explore the importance of building a diverse and inclusive business and discuss strategies for entrepreneurs to achieve this goal.

Definition and Explanation of Diversity and Inclusion

Diversity refers to the differences in gender, age, race, ethnicity, religion, sexual orientation, education, and socioeconomic status among people. Inclusion refers to the creation of a work environment where all employees feel valued and respected, and their differences are recognized and embraced. Diversity without inclusion can create a hostile and unproductive work environment, whereas inclusion without diversity leads to homogeneity and lack of innovation. Therefore, both diversity and inclusion are crucial for a thriving business.

Building a diverse and inclusive business has numerous benefits, including:

Improved creativity and innovation: Diverse teams bring different perspectives and experiences to the table, leading to new and innovative ideas.

Better problem-solving: Diverse teams can approach problems from multiple angles, leading to more effective solutions.

Improved employee engagement and retention: When employees feel valued and respected, they are more likely to be engaged and less likely to leave the organization.

Improved customer satisfaction: A diverse workforce can better understand and serve a diverse customer base.

Increased profitability: A study by McKinsey & Company found that companies in the top quartile for gender diversity on executive teams were 21% more likely to have above-average profitability than companies in the bottom quartile.

Strategies for Building a Diverse and Inclusive Business :

Create a culture of inclusion: A culture of inclusion starts at the top. Leaders must model inclusive behaviors and language and hold all employees accountable for doing the same. This includes creating a safe and welcoming work environment where all employees feel comfortable sharing their ideas and opinions.

Remove bias from the hiring process: Unconscious bias can affect the hiring process, leading to the exclusion of qualified candidates. To mitigate this, entrepreneurs can implement blind resume reviews, diverse interview panels, and standardized interview questions.

Develop a diversity and inclusion strategy: Entrepreneurs should develop a diversity and inclusion strategy that outlines specific goals and objectives for the organization. This strategy should include initiatives for recruiting, hiring, promoting, and retaining a diverse workforce.

Provide diversity and inclusion training: Providing diversity and inclusion training to all employees can help raise awareness of unconscious bias and promote inclusive behaviors.

Foster employee resource groups: Employee resource groups (ERGs) can provide a supportive and inclusive environment for employees with shared experiences or backgrounds. Entrepreneurs can support the formation and growth of ERGs to promote diversity and inclusion in the workplace.

Offer flexible work arrangements: Offering flexible work arrangements, such as remote work or flexible hours, can promote inclusion by accommodating the diverse needs of employees.

Implement inclusive policies and practices: Entrepreneurs can implement policies and practices that support diversity and inclusion, such as equal pay, parental leave, and accommodations for employees with disabilities.

Partner with diverse suppliers: Entrepreneurs can promote diversity and inclusion in their supply chain by partnering with diverse suppliers. This can include minority-owned businesses, women-owned businesses, and businesses owned by members of the LGBTQ+ community.

Challenges of Building a Diverse and Inclusive Business

Building a diverse and inclusive business is not without its challenges. Some of the common challenges entrepreneurs may face include:

Resistance to change: Some employees may be resistant to change or. feel uncomfortable with new policies or practices aimed at promoting diversity and inclusion. This resistance can stem from fear of the unknown, fear of losing power or privilege, or simply a lack of understanding or awareness. Overcoming this resistance requires strong leadership, effective communication, and a commitment to ongoing education and training.

Unconscious biases: Everyone has unconscious biases, or preconceived ideas and attitudes that influence our perceptions and decision-making processes without us even realizing it. These biases can lead to discrimination and exclusion in hiring, promotion, and other business practices. Overcoming unconscious biases requires self-awareness, education, and a willingness to challenge our assumptions and stereotypes.

Lack of diversity in the talent pool: In some industries, the talent pool may not be as diverse as we would like it to be. This can make it difficult to build a diverse and inclusive workforce, especially if there is strong competition for qualified candidates. Overcoming this challenge requires creativity and a willingness to look beyond traditional recruitment channels, as well as efforts to develop and train a more diverse talent pipeline.

Unequal access to resources: In many cases, marginalized groups may have less access to the resources and networks that are essential for building a successful business. This can include access to funding, mentorship, professional networks, and other forms of support. Overcoming this challenge requires a commitment to equity and inclusion, as well as efforts to level the playing field through targeted outreach and support.

Inadequate support systems: Building a diverse and inclusive business requires ongoing effort and resources. It requires leaders who are committed to the cause, and it requires employees who are willing to challenge their own biases and assumptions. Without adequate support systems in place, it can be difficult to sustain these efforts over time. Overcoming this challenge requires a commitment to ongoing education and training, as well as the creation of supportive policies and practices that promote diversity and inclusion at all levels of the organization.

Conclusion

Building a successful business is never easy, but building a diverse and inclusive business can be especially challenging. It requires a deep commitment to equity and inclusion, as well as a willingness to challenge our assumptions and biases. It requires leaders who are willing to take risks and embrace change, and employees who are willing to learn and grow.

But the rewards of building a diverse and inclusive business are significant. By creating a culture of belonging and respect, we can attract and retain top talent, foster innovation and creativity, and build stronger relationships with customers and communities. We can also help to promote social justice and equity, and contribute to a more just and equitable society.

Ultimately, building a diverse and inclusive business is not just good for business—it's good for people, and for our world. As entrepreneurs and business leaders, we have a unique opportunity to make a positive impact on the world around us. Let's seize that opportunity, and build a more diverse, inclusive, and just future for all.

Marketing and Branding

Marketing and branding are critical components of building a successful business. Marketing refers to the activities involved in promoting and selling a product or service, while branding refers to the creation of a unique identity for a business.

Entrepreneurs should understand the importance of developing a marketing strategy that is in line with their business goals and target market. This can involve researching your target market and their preferences, as well as identifying the most effective marketing channels to reach them.

Branding is also critical to the success of a business. Entrepreneurs should focus on creating a unique brand identity that sets their business apart from others in the market. This can involve creating a logo, tagline, and visual style that reflect the values and personality of the business. Entrepreneurs should also consider how they want their customers to perceive their business, and work to build a consistent brand image across all marketing materials and channels.

In addition to traditional marketing channels, such as advertising and direct mail, entrepreneurs should also consider digital marketing strategies. This can include creating a website, utilizing social media, and developing a search engine optimization (SEO) strategy.

Ultimately, entrepreneurs should view marketing and branding as ongoing efforts, and be prepared to continually adapt and evolve their strategies over time as their business grows and evolves. By developing a strong marketing and branding strategy, entrepreneurs can build a strong reputation and attract new customers and business opportunities.

Marketing and branding are critical components of any business strategy. They help to communicate the value and uniqueness of your product or service, and to differentiate your business from your competitors. Here are some key tips and considerations for developing an effective marketing and branding strategy:

- Identify your target audience: Identifying your target audience is critical for developing an effective marketing and branding strategy. Understanding your target audience's needs, preferences, and behaviors can help you to tailor your messaging, positioning, and offerings to better meet their needs.
- Develop a unique brand identity: A unique brand identity is essential for differentiating your business from your competitors. Be sure to develop a clear and consistent brand image, message, and tone, and to use these elements consistently across all of your marketing and branding efforts.
- Utilize multiple channels: Utilizing multiple channels is important for reaching your target audience and building your brand. Be sure to consider a variety of channels, such as social media, email marketing, content marketing, and advertising, and to develop a comprehensive, integrated marketing plan.
- Measure and analyze your results: Measuring and analyzing your results is critical for improving your marketing and branding efforts. Be sure to track your results and to continuously refine your strategy based on your findings.
- Engage your audience: Engaging your audience is important for building brand loyalty and advocacy. Encourage your audience to participate in your marketing and branding efforts

Understanding the Importance of Marketing

Marketing is a critical component of any successful business. It is the process of promoting and selling products or services through a variety of communication channels. Understanding the importance of marketing is crucial for entrepreneurs looking to launch and grow their business. Here's why.

- Helps you reach your target audience: Marketing allows you to reach the people who are most likely to be interested in your products or services. By understanding your target market and using the right marketing strategies, you can reach your ideal customers and build strong relationships with them.
- Increases brand awareness: Marketing helps increase brand awareness by promoting your business and its products or services to the public. This can help you stand out from your competition and make a lasting impression on potential customers.
- Boosts sales and revenue: Marketing can help you increase your sales and revenue by attracting more customers to your business. Through effective marketing strategies, you can reach more people, generate more leads, and convert more of those leads into sales.
- Enhances customer engagement: Marketing can also help you engage with your customers and build stronger relationships with them. By providing valuable content, responding to customer questions and feedback, and offering personalized experiences, you can create a loyal customer base that is more likely to return and recommend your business to others.
- Helps you stay competitive: In today's fast-paced business world, it's essential to stay ahead of the competition. Marketing can help you do this by keeping your business top-of-mind with customers and ensuring that your products and services are meeting their needs and expectations.

In conclusion, marketing is a vital part of growing and sustaining a successful business. By understanding the importance of marketing and using effective marketing strategies, you can reach your target audience, increase brand awareness, boost sales and revenue, enhance customer engagement, and stay competitive in your industry.

Developing a Marketing Strategy

Developing a marketing strategy is an essential step for any business looking to build brand awareness, increase customer engagement, and drive sales. A well-crafted marketing strategy helps you define your target audience, determine your unique selling proposition, and establish a clear plan for promoting your products or services. Here's a closer look at the importance of developing a marketing strategy.

- Defines your target audience: A marketing strategy helps you identify your target audience and understand their needs, preferences, and behaviors. This information is crucial in determining the best approach to reach and engage your target customers.
- Establishes your unique selling proposition: A marketing strategy helps you define your unique selling proposition, which is what sets your business apart from your competition. This information can help you create messaging that resonates with your target audience and differentiates your business from others in the market.
- Aligns marketing activities with business goals: A marketing strategy provides a roadmap for your marketing activities and ensures that they align with your overall business goals. This can help you stay focused on the outcomes that matter most to your business and avoid wasting resources on ineffective marketing efforts.
- Maximizes the impact of marketing efforts: A well-crafted marketing strategy helps you maximize the impact of your marketing efforts by identifying the channels that are most effective for reaching your target audience. This information can help you allocate resources to the channels that are most likely to deliver results and optimize your marketing spend.
- Facilitates measurement and evaluation: A marketing strategy provides a framework for measuring the success of your marketing efforts and evaluating the impact of different marketing activities on your business goals. This information

is critical in making informed decisions about how to optimize your marketing efforts over time.

In conclusion, developing a marketing strategy is an essential step for any business looking to build brand awareness, increase customer engagement, and drive sales. By defining your target audience, establishing your unique selling proposition, aligning marketing activities with business goals, maximizing the impact of your marketing efforts, and facilitating measurement and evaluation, you can ensure that your marketing efforts are effective, efficient, and delivering the results you need to grow your business.

Building a Strong Brand Identity

Building a strong brand identity is a crucial step in establishing a successful business. A strong brand identity helps to differentiate a business from its competitors and creates a memorable and recognizable image in the minds of customers.

To build a strong brand identity, entrepreneurs should start by considering the values and personality of their business. What makes their business unique? What do they want their customers to think of when they hear the name of their business? This can help entrepreneurs to identify key themes and messaging to include in their branding efforts.

Next, entrepreneurs should focus on creating a visual style for their brand. This can include designing a logo, tagline, and color palette that reflect the personality and values of their business. It is important to keep these elements consistent across all marketing materials, including business cards, websites, and social media accounts.

In addition to visual elements, entrepreneurs should also focus on building a consistent brand voice. This can involve creating guidelines for tone, language, and messaging that should be used across all marketing materials.

Finally, entrepreneurs should consider how they can integrate their brand into the customer experience. This can include creating a consistent look and feel in their physical storefront, as well as ensuring that customer interactions, such as phone and email communications, align with their brand image and messaging.

By taking a thoughtful and strategic approach to building a strong brand identity, entrepreneurs can establish a memorable and recognizable image for their business that helps to attract new customers and build loyalty among existing ones.

A strong brand identity is a critical component of success for any business. A well-defined brand identity sets your business apart from competitors and helps you establish a strong connection with your target audience. Here's a closer look at the importance of building a strong brand identity and how to do it.

- Creates a memorable impression: A strong brand identity creates a memorable impression on your target audience, which helps you stand out in a crowded marketplace. This can help you build brand recognition and foster loyalty among customers.
- Conveys your values and personality: A strong brand identity conveys the values and personality of your business, which helps you establish a connection with your target audience. By creating a brand identity that reflects the unique personality and values of your business, you can create a strong emotional connection with customers that will help drive engagement and sales.
- Supports brand consistency: A strong brand identity helps ensure brand consistency across all of your marketing materials and customer touchpoints. This can help you build brand recognition and establish a consistent image in the minds of your target audience.
- Enhances credibility: A well-defined brand identity can enhance the credibility of your business, especially if it is professional, consistent, and in line with the expectations of your target audience.
- Facilitates growth: A strong brand identity can facilitate growth for your business by making it easier to attract new customers and expand into new markets.
- To build a strong brand identity, consider the following steps:
- Define your brand values and personality: Start by defining the values and personality of your business and make sure that these are reflected in your brand identity.
- Conduct market research: Conduct market research to understand the expectations and preferences of your target audience, and use this information to inform your brand identity.
- Create a brand strategy: Develop a brand strategy that defines the core elements of your brand identity, such as your brand mission, vision, and values.
- Develop a visual identity: Create a visual identity that includes a logo, color palette, and typography that reflects the personality and values of your brand.
- Ensure brand consistency: Make sure that your brand identity is consistent across all of your marketing materials and customer touchpoints.

Building a Strong Online Presence

Building a Strong Online Presence is a crucial aspect of growing and scaling a business in today's digital age. In this section, you could explore the various ways entrepreneurs can establish and maintain a strong online presence, from creating a website and social media accounts to developing a content marketing strategy and leveraging search engine optimization (SEO) techniques.

Entrepreneurs can also use online platforms to reach and engage with their target audience, build brand awareness, and generate leads and sales. In this section, we are discussing the importance of creating valuable and relevant content, such as blog posts, videos, and infographics, that provides value to your audience and positions your business as a thought leader in your industry.

Additionally, this section could touch on the importance of tracking and analyzing your online presence to understand how your audience is interacting with your content and making data-driven decisions to improve your online presence over time.

The Building a Strong Online Presence section aims to help entrepreneurs understand the importance of having a strong online presence and the various strategies and tactics they can use to establish and maintain one. By building a strong online presence, entrepreneurs can reach and engage with a wider audience, build brand awareness, and drive business growth.

Having a strong online presence is essential for entrepreneurs to succeed in today's digital world. A strong online presence can help entrepreneurs reach a wider audience, build brand awareness, generate leads and sales, and grow their business.

One of the first steps in building a strong online presence is to create a website and social media accounts. A website is a virtual storefront for your business, and social media accounts can be used to connect with your target audience and share content.

Content marketing is another crucial aspect of building a strong online presence. By creating valuable and relevant content, such as blog posts, videos, and infographics, and etc.

Content marketing can also help drive traffic to your website and increase your search engine ranking, making it easier for potential customers to find you online.

Search engine optimization (SEO) is also an important strategy for building a strong online presence. By optimizing your website and content for search engines, you can improve your visibility and increase the likelihood that potential customers will find you when they search for related products or services online.

In addition to creating a website and social media accounts, entrepreneurs can also use online platforms such as email marketing, pay-per-click advertising, and influencer marketing to reach and engage with their target audience. Email marketing can be used to stay in touch with your subscribers and promote your products or services, while pay-per-click advertising can help drive targeted traffic to your website. Influencer marketing can be used to partner with influencers in your industry and leverage their following to reach a wider audience.

It's also important for entrepreneurs to track and analyze their online presence to understand how their audience is interacting with their content and make data-driven decisions to improve their online presence over time. This can be done through tools such as Google Analytics, which provides insights into your website traffic and audience behavior.

Let's delve into the topic of building a strong online presence for e-commerce businesses.

An e-commerce business's online presence is critical for its success as it provides a platform for customers to purchase products and services. A strong online presence can help e-commerce businesses reach a wider audience, build brand awareness, generate leads and sales, and grow their business.

Here are a few key strategies for building a strong online presence for e-commerce businesses:

- Create a user-friendly e-commerce website: The e-commerce website should be well-designed and easy to navigate, with clear and concise product descriptions and high-quality product images. The website should also be optimized for mobile devices, as an increasing number of consumers are using their smartphones to make online purchases.
- Utilize social media platforms: Social media platforms such as Facebook, Instagram, and Twitter can be used to reach a wider audience and build brand

awareness. E-commerce businesses can use these platforms to share product updates, offer promotions, and interact with their target audience.

- Leverage email marketing: Email marketing is an effective way to stay in touch with customers and promote products and services. E-commerce businesses can use email marketing to share product updates, offer promotions, and drive sales.
- Implement search engine optimization (SEO) techniques: SEO is the process of optimizing your website and content to improve your visibility in search engine results pages. This is critical for e-commerce businesses as it can help drive traffic to their website and increase their search engine ranking, making it easier for potential customers to find them online.
- Offer free shipping and returns: Free shipping and returns can be a powerful motivator for customers to make a purchase, especially for e-commerce businesses that are just starting out. Offering free shipping and returns can help increase conversions and build customer loyalty.
- Use customer reviews and ratings: Customer reviews and ratings can be a powerful tool for e-commerce businesses to build trust with their target audience. By showcasing positive customer reviews and ratings, e-commerce businesses can demonstrate the quality of their products and services and encourage potential customers to make a purchase.

In conclusion, building a strong online presence is critical for e-commerce businesses to succeed in today's digital age. By implementing these strategies, e-commerce businesses can reach and engage with their target audience, build brand awareness, and drive business growth.

Managing Your Finances

Managing your finances is a critical aspect of running a successful business. It involves keeping track of your income, expenses, and cash flow to make informed decisions that support your business goals and keep you financially stable. A strong financial foundation is essential to achieve long-term success in entrepreneurship. In this section of "Fuel Your Dreams: A Guide to Fueling Entrepreneurship", you'll learn about the importance of managing your finances and some of the key elements involved.

The first step in managing your finances is to understand financial statements. This includes balance sheets, income statements, and cash flow statements, which provide a comprehensive view of your business's financial health. Understanding these statements is crucial for making informed decisions about how to allocate resources and manage your budget.

Another critical aspect of managing your finances is budgeting and cash flow management. This involves projecting your income and expenses, as well as tracking actual results to ensure that you're staying on course. Proper budgeting and cash flow management can help you avoid financial difficulties and ensure that you have sufficient funds to invest in growth opportunities.

it's essential to be mindful of taxation and legal requirements when managing your finances. This involves understanding and complying with local, state, and federal laws and regulations, as well as paying taxes in a timely manner. Failure to comply with these requirements can result in significant financial penalties, so it's important to be proactive and informed.

Managing your finances is an essential aspect of running a successful business. Whether you are a startup or an established company, having a solid financial plan and implementing effective financial management practices can help you achieve your business goals and ensure long-term success. Here's a closer look at the importance of managing your finances and some tips for doing it effectively.

- Helps you make informed decisions: Effective financial management helps you make informed decisions about your business by providing you with a clear picture of your financial position and future prospects. This information can help you make informed decisions about investing in new initiatives, expanding your operations, and more.
- Supports cash flow management: Effective financial management is crucial in ensuring that your business has sufficient cash flow to meet its obligations and invest in growth. This can help you avoid financial problems and ensure that your business is in a strong financial position.
- Facilitates budgeting and forecasting: Effective financial management helps you create and stick to a budget, which is essential in managing your expenses and maximizing your profits. It also enables you to create accurate financial forecasts that can help you plan for the future and make informed decisions about your business.
- Helps you identify areas for improvement: Regular financial management and analysis can help you identify areas for improvement in your business operations and make necessary changes to optimize your financial performance.

In conclusion, managing your finances is an essential part of running a successful business. It requires a comprehensive understanding of financial statements, budgeting and cash flow management, as well as compliance with taxation and legal requirements. By prioritizing your financial health, you can ensure that your business is well-positioned for long-term success.

Understanding Financial Statements

As an entrepreneur, it is important to have a basic understanding of financial statements in order to make informed business decisions and accurately track the financial health of your company. Financial statements provide a snapshot of your company's financial position and help you monitor its progress over time.

There are three main financial statements that every entrepreneur should be familiar with: the balance sheet, the income statement, and the cash flow statement.

The balance sheet provides a snapshot of a company's financial position at a specific point in time. It lists all of the company's assets, liabilities, and equity. Assets include things like cash, inventory, and property. Liabilities are debts that the company owes to others, such as loans or accounts payable. Equity is the portion of the company that is owned by its shareholders, and it represents the residual interest in the assets of the company after liabilities have been subtracted.

The income statement shows a company's revenue, expenses, and net profit or loss over a specific period of time, typically a month or a year. Revenue represents the money a company earns from selling its products or services, while expenses are the costs associated with running the business. The net profit or loss is the difference between revenue and expenses.

The cash flow statement shows the inflows and outflows of cash over a specific period of time. It shows where cash came from, where it went, and how it was used. This statement is particularly important for entrepreneurs because it helps them understand whether their company is generating enough cash to pay its bills, invest in new opportunities, and continue operating.

In order to make informed business decisions, it is important to regularly review and analyze these financial statements. This can help you identify trends, assess performance, and make changes as needed. A basic understanding of financial statements can also help you communicate effectively with investors, lenders, and other stakeholders who are interested in your company's financial health.

In conclusion, as an entrepreneur, understanding financial statements is a critical component of successful business management. By regularly reviewing and analyzing these statements, you can make informed decisions, monitor your company's financial health, and communicate effectively with stakeholders.

Budgeting and Cash Flow Management

Budgeting and cash flow management are essential components of any successful business. These processes help entrepreneurs ensure that their businesses have the resources they need to operate effectively and grow over time. Here's a closer look at the importance of budgeting and cash flow management.

- Helps you prioritize spending: Budgeting allows you to plan for the future by allocating resources to the areas of your business that are most important. By creating a budget, you can identify your income and expenses, determine which expenses are essential, and prioritize your spending to ensure that your business has the resources it needs to succeed.

- Improves financial stability: By keeping a close eye on your cash flow, you can identify potential financial problems before they become major issues. This can help you avoid financial crises, such as running out of money, and improve the overall stability of your business.

- Facilitates long-term planning: Budgeting and cash flow management also help you plan for the future by giving you a clear picture of your financial situation. This can help you make informed decisions about the future of your business, such as investing in new products or services, expanding into new markets, or hiring additional employees.

- Supports informed decision-making: Budgeting and cash flow management provide you with important information that can help you make informed decisions about your business. For example, by monitoring your cash flow, you can identify areas where you may need to reduce expenses, such as reducing inventory levels or negotiating better deals with suppliers.

- Increases accountability: By creating and adhering to a budget, you increase accountability within your business. This can help you make sure that everyone is working together towards common goals and that resources are being used in the most efficient way possible.

In conclusion, budgeting and cash flow management are critical components of any successful business. By using these tools, you can prioritize spending, improve financial stability, facilitate long-term planning, support informed decision-making, and increase accountability within your organization.

Managing Taxation and Legal Requirements

As a business owner, it's important to understand and properly manage the various tax and legal requirements that apply to your business. Failing to comply with these requirements can result in significant financial penalties, legal consequences, and damage to your reputation.

When it comes to taxes, it's essential to understand the various tax obligations for your business, including income tax, sales tax, payroll taxes, and any other taxes that may apply to your specific business model. You should also be familiar with the tax laws and regulations in your jurisdiction, including the deadlines for filing tax returns and paying taxes.

In terms of legal requirements, there are a variety of laws and regulations that can impact your business, such as employment laws, consumer protection laws, and health and safety regulations. It's important to be aware of these laws and to take steps to ensure that your business is in compliance. This may include seeking the advice of a lawyer or consulting with a business advisor.

In order to manage your taxes and legal requirements effectively, it's important to keep accurate financial records and to stay organized. This can include keeping detailed records of your income and expenses, as well as any other financial transactions that are relevant to your business.

Taxation
The first step to managing your tax obligations is to understand what types of taxes you'll be required to pay. This will vary depending on your business structure, location, and income. Common taxes for businesses include income tax, sales tax, and payroll tax. You'll also need to keep records of your income and expenses to accurately calculate your tax liability.

Legal Requirements

In addition to taxes, there are also a number of legal requirements that businesses must comply with. These can include registering your business, obtaining necessary licenses and permits, and protecting your intellectual property through trademarks and patents. You may also need to comply with workplace health and safety regulations, data protection laws, and environmental regulations.

Consult with an Expert

Navigating the complex world of taxation and legal requirements can be challenging, so it's a good idea to consult with a tax professional or attorney. They can help you understand your obligations and ensure that you're meeting all requirements. Additionally, they can provide guidance on tax planning and help you minimize your tax liability.

Stay Up-to-Date

The world of taxation and legal requirements is constantly changing, so it's important to stay informed and up-to-date on the latest regulations and requirements. This may involve regularly reviewing your business's structure, reviewing changes to tax laws, and ensuring that your employees are trained on the latest regulations and requirements.

In conclusion, managing taxation and legal requirements is an important aspect of running a successful business. By understanding your obligations, staying informed, and seeking expert advice, you can ensure that your business is in compliance with all regulations and on the path to success.

Navigating Challenges and Overcoming Obstacles

Starting and running a business can be a challenging journey, and entrepreneurs need to be prepared to face a variety of obstacles along the way. Some common challenges faced by entrepreneurs include:

- Cash flow management: Many startups struggle to manage their finances and maintain a positive cash flow.
- Competition: Entrepreneurs need to be aware of their competitors and find ways to differentiate themselves from them.
- Regulatory compliance: Entrepreneurs must navigate a complex web of laws and regulations, including those related to taxation, labor, and environmental protection.
- Hiring and retaining talent: Finding and retaining top talent can be a major challenge for entrepreneurs, especially in highly competitive industries.
- Scaling the business: As a business grows, entrepreneurs must find ways to maintain its growth while also managing operational costs and other challenges. To overcome these obstacles, entrepreneurs must develop resilience, adaptability, and a strong support system. This can include seeking out mentors, joining entrepreneur networks, and taking advantage of resources like business incubators and accelerators. Additionally, it is important for entrepreneurs to take time to reflect on their journey, celebrate their accomplishments, and continue to learn and grow as business owners. By approaching challenges with a positive attitude and a growth mindset, entrepreneurs can navigate the ups and downs of starting and running a business and achieve their long-term goals.

As an entrepreneur, you'll likely face a number of challenges and obstacles along the way. Whether it's competition, changes in the market, or unexpected setbacks, it's important to have a plan for overcoming these obstacles. Here are a few key strategies for navigating challenges and overcoming obstacles:

Stay Adaptable
One of the keys to success as an entrepreneur is being adaptable. The world of business is constantly changing, and it's important to be able to change with it. This may involve being open to new ideas, being willing to pivot your business strategy, and being flexible in your approach.

Develop Resilience
Resilience is an important trait for entrepreneurs. You'll likely face setbacks and challenges along the way, and it's important to be able to bounce back from these challenges. This may involve developing a growth mindset, being persistent in the face of setbacks, and having a positive outlook.

Build a Support Network
Another important strategy for overcoming challenges is to build a support network. This may involve seeking out mentorship, networking with other entrepreneurs, and building a team of employees who share your vision and values.

In conclusion, navigating challenges and overcoming obstacles is an important part of being an entrepreneur. By staying adaptable, developing resilience, and building a strong support network, you can increase your chances of success and build a business that lasts.

Common Challenges Faced by Entrepreneurs

Starting and growing a business is not an easy task, and entrepreneurs often face a variety of challenges along the way. Some of the most common challenges faced by entrepreneurs include:

- Lack of funding: Many entrepreneurs struggle to secure the funding they need to get their business off the ground. This can be due to a lack of assets, a lack of a proven track record, or simply a lack of interest from investors.
- Competition: Entrepreneurs often find themselves competing against well-established businesses with more resources, which can make it difficult to establish a foothold in the market.
- Finding and retaining customers: Attracting and retaining customers is one of the biggest challenges facing entrepreneurs. This can involve developing a strong marketing strategy, building a strong brand, and providing high-quality products or services that meet the needs of customers.
- Hiring and managing employees: Entrepreneurs must often hire and manage employees, which can be a complex and time-consuming task. Finding the right people, providing them with the right training and support, and ensuring they are motivated and engaged are critical components of success.
- Navigating legal and regulatory requirements: Entrepreneurs must often navigate complex legal and regulatory requirements, such as obtaining necessary licenses and permits, protecting intellectual property, and complying with labor laws.
- Balancing work and personal life: Many entrepreneurs find it difficult to balance the demands of running a business with the demands of their personal life. This can lead to burnout and other physical and mental health issues.

Despite these challenges, many entrepreneurs are able to overcome them by developing strong business skills, seeking support from mentors and peers, and staying focused on their goals. By staying persistent and resilient, entrepreneurs can find success and achieve their dreams.

Developing Resilience and Adaptability

As an entrepreneur, it's inevitable that you'll face challenges and obstacles along the way. However, the key to success is how you handle those challenges and how you adapt to them. Developing resilience and adaptability are crucial skills that every entrepreneur must possess to overcome these challenges and achieve their goals.

Resilience refers to an individual's ability to bounce back from adversity, setbacks, and challenges. It's about having the mental toughness to persevere through difficult times and come out stronger on the other side. Entrepreneurs with high levels of resilience are better equipped to handle stress and challenges, and are more likely to succeed in their ventures.

Adaptability, on the other hand, refers to an individual's ability to change and adjust to new and changing circumstances. Entrepreneurs need to be adaptable in order to respond to market changes, shifts in consumer behavior, and other external factors that can affect their business. Adaptable entrepreneurs are able to pivot their strategy, adjust their approach, and find new solutions to problems, which is essential for success in a rapidly changing business environment.

So, how can entrepreneurs develop resilience and adaptability? Here are a few tips:

- Embrace change: Embracing change and uncertainty is an important part of developing adaptability. Entrepreneurs need to be comfortable with ambiguity and be willing to take calculated risks in order to drive their business forward.
- Learn from failures: Instead of viewing failures as setbacks, entrepreneurs can learn from them and use that knowledge to make better decisions in the future. This helps to build resilience and the ability to bounce back from adversity.
- Seek support: Entrepreneurs should build a supportive network of friends, family, and colleagues who can provide encouragement and guidance during difficult times.

- Stay positive: Maintaining a positive attitude and a growth mindset can help entrepreneurs stay motivated and focused during challenging times.
- Practice self-care: Taking care of oneself, both physically and mentally, is essential for building resilience. Regular exercise, healthy eating, and engaging in stress-relieving activities like meditation or yoga can help entrepreneurs stay in top form.

In conclusion, developing resilience and adaptability is a crucial part of entrepreneurial success. By embracing change, learning from failures, seeking support, staying positive, and practicing self-care, entrepreneurs can build the mental toughness and flexibility they need to overcome challenges and achieve their goals.

Seeking Support and Mentorship

Starting and running a business can be a challenging and demanding journey. However, seeking support and mentorship can greatly enhance an entrepreneur's chances of success. By leveraging the experience and expertise of others, entrepreneurs can navigate obstacles, make informed decisions, and grow their business more effectively.

Seeking Support: One of the key benefits of seeking support as an entrepreneur is access to a network of individuals who have gone through the same challenges and can offer valuable insights and advice. Joining a local entrepreneur or business organization can provide a supportive community and a platform for exchanging ideas and resources. In addition, entrepreneurs can turn to family and friends for support, as well as professional services such as business coaches and consultants.

Mentorship: Another valuable aspect of seeking support is the opportunity to find a mentor. Mentors are individuals with significant experience and expertise in a particular field who offer guidance and advice to entrepreneurs. They can provide advice on various business aspects, such as marketing, finance, and operations, and help entrepreneurs avoid common pitfalls and make better decisions.

Benefits of Mentorship: Having a mentor can provide entrepreneurs with a sounding board for their ideas and a source of inspiration. Mentors can help entrepreneurs stay focused and motivated, provide valuable feedback, and introduce them to key contacts and opportunities. In addition, mentorship relationships can provide a valuable opportunity for personal and professional growth.

Choosing a Mentor: When choosing a mentor, it is important to consider their expertise, experience, and personality. Entrepreneurs should look for mentors who are knowledgeable, trustworthy, and invested in their success. Building a relationship with a mentor takes time and effort, so it is important to select someone who is a good fit and who is committed to the partnership.

In conclusion, seeking support and mentorship can play a crucial role in the success of a business. Entrepreneurs who are looking to scale and grow their business can benefit from the guidance and advice of experienced individuals who can provide valuable insights and support along the way.

Entrepreneurial Burnout and Self-Care

The Entrepreneurial Burnout and Self-Care section aims to help entrepreneurs understand the importance of taking care of themselves and avoiding burnout. By recognizing the signs of burnout and taking proactive steps to prevent it, entrepreneurs can maintain their health and wellbeing and increase their chances of success in their entrepreneurial journey.

Entrepreneurship is a demanding and challenging path that requires not only hard work and dedication, but also a focus on self-care and wellness. The demands of running a business can lead to high levels of stress and burnout, which can have serious negative impacts on an entrepreneur's health and overall success.

Self-care is a crucial component of avoiding burnout for entrepreneurs. This includes setting clear boundaries between work and personal time, practicing mindfulness and relaxation techniques, and engaging in regular physical activity. Seeking support and mentorship is also important, as it can help entrepreneurs manage stress and maintain a healthy work-life balance.

Entrepreneurship can bring about a unique set of demands and challenges that can take a toll on one's mental and physical health. For example, entrepreneurs often work long hours, deal with constant pressure to succeed, and make critical decisions that can impact their business and their lives. All of these demands can lead to high levels of stress and eventually, burnout.

It's crucial for entrepreneurs to be aware of the signs and symptoms of burnout and take proactive steps to prevent it. Some of the common signs of burnout include feeling exhausted and drained, feeling disconnected from one's work, decreased motivation and productivity, and a sense of cynicism or detachment from one's business. Recognizing these symptoms early on is key to taking action and avoiding burnout.

Self-care is one of the most effective ways for entrepreneurs to prevent burnout. This includes engaging in activities that promote physical and mental wellbeing, such as regular exercise, eating a balanced diet, getting enough sleep, and practicing mindfulness and relaxation techniques. It's also important to set clear boundaries between work and personal time to avoid overworking and feeling overwhelmed.

In addition to self-care, seeking support and mentorship can also help entrepreneurs prevent burnout. Having a support network, whether it is a mentor, coach, or group of fellow entrepreneurs, can provide a sounding board for ideas and help entrepreneurs process their experiences and challenges. This can help entrepreneurs stay motivated, manage stress, and maintain a healthy work-life balance.

Furthermore, entrepreneurs can also benefit from seeking therapy or counseling services to help them navigate the demands and challenges of entrepreneurship. Talking to a professional can provide a safe and supportive space for entrepreneurs to process their thoughts and feelings, and develop coping strategies to manage stress and prevent burnout.

In conclusion, entrepreneurial burnout is a serious concern for entrepreneurs, but it is preventable. By being aware of the signs and symptoms of burnout and taking proactive steps to prioritize self-care and seek support, entrepreneurs can maintain their health and wellbeing, increase their chances of success, and enjoy a more fulfilling and sustainable entrepreneurial journey.

Time Management and Productivity

Time Management and Productivity is an essential aspect of entrepreneurship. With the multitude of tasks and responsibilities that entrepreneurs face, it's critical to be efficient and effective with their time.

In this section, we discuss the various time management techniques and strategies that entrepreneurs can use to maximize your productivity, such as prioritizing tasks, delegating responsibilities, and avoiding distractions. Additionally, this section could explore the use of technology and tools, such as task management software and productivity apps, to help entrepreneurs stay organized and on track.

Furthermore, this section is touching on the importance of setting realistic goals and breaking down large projects into smaller, manageable tasks. By doing so, entrepreneurs can avoid feeling overwhelmed and can make steady progress towards their goals.

Moreover, this section emphasizing the importance of taking breaks and maintaining a healthy work-life balance, which can help entrepreneurs stay energized and focused. By managing their time and maximizing their productivity, entrepreneurs can achieve more in less time and increase their chances of success in their entrepreneurial journey.

Prioritizing tasks is the process of identifying and organizing tasks based on their level of importance and urgency. In the context of time management for entrepreneurs, it means focusing on the most critical tasks that need immediate attention to achieve their business goals.

To prioritize tasks effectively, entrepreneurs must first set specific and measurable goals. They should then assess which tasks are most critical to achieving these goals, considering factors such as deadlines, impact on the business, and potential risks or consequences.

Entrepreneurs should then allocate their time and resources based on the level of priority of each task. They can do this by scheduling their workday, creating to-do lists, and using productivity tools such as calendars and task management software. By prioritizing tasks, entrepreneurs can focus on the most important and impactful activities, which can lead to better results and increased productivity.

Delegating responsibilities refers to the process of assigning tasks to other team members or employees. It is an essential strategy for entrepreneurs to effectively manage their time and focus on more critical tasks that require their attention. By delegating tasks, entrepreneurs can free up their time and prioritize their work more efficiently.

Delegating responsibilities requires effective communication, trust, and clear expectations. Entrepreneurs need to communicate the importance of the delegated tasks, provide clear instructions, and establish specific deadlines. They should also ensure that the team members responsible for completing the tasks have the necessary skills and resources to complete them successfully.

To delegate effectively, entrepreneurs should trust their team members and allow them to take ownership of their tasks. This can increase motivation and productivity while allowing entrepreneurs to focus on more sign ificant business issues. It is also crucial to provide feedback and recognize the efforts of the team members who have successfully completed the delegated tasks.

In summary, delegation is a critical strategy for entrepreneurs to manage their time effectively and increase productivity. By assigning tasks to other team members and employees, entrepreneurs can focus on more critical tasks while ensuring that all tasks are completed efficiently and on time. Effective delegation requires clear communication, trust, and establishing clear expectations, as well as providing feedback and recognition to the team members responsible for completing the tasks.

Avoiding distractions is a critical aspect of time management and productivity for entrepreneurs. Distractions such as social media, emails, and phone calls can consume valuable time and distract entrepreneurs from completing critical tasks.

To avoid distractions, entrepreneurs need to prioritize their work and create a distraction-free work environment. This involves setting clear goals and deadlines and focusing on completing the most critical tasks first. Entrepreneurs can use productivity tools, such as task lists or calendars, to stay organized and focused.

Creating a distraction-free work environment involves eliminating or minimizing potential distractions. For example, entrepreneurs can turn off notifications on their phones or computers, schedule specific times to check emails or social media, and limit non-work-related activities during work hours. They can also choose to work in a quiet, dedicated workspace or use noise-cancelling headphones to block out external noise.

Avoiding distractions can help entrepreneurs stay focused and productive, which can lead to better results and increased success in their business ventures. By prioritizing their work and creating a distraction-free work environment, entrepreneurs can make the most of their time and increase their chances of achieving their goals.

The use of technology and tools is an essential aspect of time management and productivity for entrepreneurs. Task management software and productivity apps are among the most useful tools available to help entrepreneurs stay organized and on track.

Task management software allows entrepreneurs to create, assign, and track tasks in one centralized location. It can help entrepreneurs stay on top of deadlines, monitor progress, and manage their schedules efficiently. Task management software can also help entrepreneurs prioritize tasks, delegate responsibilities, and collaborate with team members.

Productivity apps are another useful tool that entrepreneurs can use to manage their time effectively. These apps can assist entrepreneurs in tracking their progress and completing tasks efficiently. For example, time-tracking apps can help entrepreneurs identify time-wasting activities and make adjustments to their work habits to increase productivity. Additionally, note-taking apps can help entrepreneurs capture ideas and organize their thoughts, while project management apps can help entrepreneurs manage large projects by breaking them down into smaller, manageable tasks.

Overall, the use of technology and tools can help entrepreneurs stay organized and on track, allowing them to make the most of their time and increase their chances of success. By utilizing task management software, productivity apps, and other technological tools, entrepreneurs can streamline their workflow, save time, and increase productivity in their business ventures.

Setting realistic goals and breaking down large projects into smaller, manageable tasks is an important aspect of time management for entrepreneurs. It can help entrepreneurs prioritize their work, stay focused, and avoid feeling overwhelmed.

By setting realistic goals, entrepreneurs can identify what they want to achieve and establish a roadmap for getting there. Setting unrealistic goals can be counterproductive, as it can lead to frustration and demotivation. Therefore, it is important for entrepreneurs to set goals that are challenging but attainable within a reasonable timeframe.

Breaking down large projects into smaller, manageable tasks is also important for entrepreneurs. Large projects can be daunting and overwhelming, making it difficult to know where to start. By breaking a project into smaller tasks, entrepreneurs can focus on one task at a time, reducing the feeling of overwhelm and making steady progress towards their goals.

Furthermore, breaking down a project into smaller tasks can help entrepreneurs identify dependencies between tasks and allocate resources effectively. By identifying the most critical tasks and allocating resources accordingly, entrepreneurs can ensure that they are making the most of their time and maximizing productivity.

In summary, setting realistic goals and breaking down large projects into smaller, manageable tasks is an important aspect of time management for entrepreneurs. It can help entrepreneurs stay focused, avoid feeling overwhelmed, and make steady progress towards their goals.

Maintaining a healthy work-life balance and taking breaks is crucial for entrepreneurs to sustain their productivity in the long term. Entrepreneurs often work long hours and face significant stress and pressure, which can lead to burnout and decreased productivity. Taking regular breaks and maintaining a healthy work-life balance can help entrepreneurs avoid burnout, stay energized and focused, and increase their overall productivity.

Regular breaks can help entrepreneurs recharge and reduce the negative effects of stress. By taking breaks, entrepreneurs can step away from their work, clear their minds, and return to their tasks with renewed energy and focus. It can also help entrepreneurs avoid decision fatigue, which can occur when the brain becomes overwhelmed by the constant need to make decisions.

Maintaining a healthy work-life balance is also essential for entrepreneurs. It can help entrepreneurs avoid burnout, reduce stress, and improve their overall quality of life. Entrepreneurs should make time for activities outside of work, such as hobbies, exercise, and spending time with family and friends. This can help entrepreneurs recharge, improve their mood, and reduce the negative effects of stress.

In summary, maintaining a healthy work-life balance and taking breaks is essential for entrepreneurs to sustain their productivity in the long term. By taking regular breaks and making time for activities outside of work, entrepreneurs can avoid burnout, stay energized and focused, and maintain their overall well-being.

In conclusion, effective time management and productivity are crucial for success as an entrepreneur. By prioritizing tasks, delegating responsibilities, avoiding distractions, using technology, setting goals, and maintaining a healthy work-life balance, entrepreneurs can increase their chances of success and achieve more in less time.

Scaling and Growing Your Business

Scaling and growing a business is an important part of entrepreneurship and can be a major challenge for many business owners. Scaling refers to the process of expanding a business, increasing its reach, and growing its impact. The goal of scaling is to create a sustainable and profitable business that can continue to grow and succeed over time.

In order to scale and grow a business, it's important to identify opportunities for expansion, such as entering new markets, launching new products, or acquiring other businesses. Entrepreneurs must also be able to effectively manage the growth process, which can include hiring and managing a larger team, managing cash flow and finances, and adapting to new challenges and obstacles.

One of the key components of scaling and growing a business is developing a sustainable business model. This involves creating a system that allows the business to operate efficiently and generate profits while also being flexible enough to adapt to changing market conditions and customer needs. A strong business model is essential for ensuring that a business can continue to grow and succeed over the long term.

Another important factor in scaling and growing a business is having a strong leadership team in place. This includes having a clear vision for the future of the business, effective decision-making processes, and the ability to motivate and inspire employees.

Finally, it's also important for entrepreneurs to continue to innovate and seek out new opportunities for growth. This may involve investing in research and development, experimenting with new business models, and embracing new technologies and marketing strategies. By staying ahead of the curve and continuously improving, entrepreneurs can ensure that their business continues to grow and succeed over time.

In conclusion, scaling and growing a business is a critical aspect of entrepreneurship that requires a combination of strategic planning, effective management, and continuous innovation. By focusing on these key areas and being proactive in seeking out new opportunities for growth, entrepreneurs can create a sustainable and profitable business that can continue to succeed over time.

Here's an example of how a business might implement strategies for scaling and growth:

ABC Consulting is a small business that provides consulting services to local businesses. After several years of steady growth, the company's CEO has decided to focus on scaling and expanding the business. Here are the steps the company takes to achieve this goal:

Identifying opportunities for expansion: The company researches potential new markets, such as nearby cities and regions, and identifies new services to offer. They also explore the option of acquiring a smaller consulting firm to increase their customer base.

Managing growth: The company hires new employees to manage increased demand for their services and sets up a more sophisticated accounting system to keep track of cash flow and finances.

Developing a sustainable business model: The company streamlines their operations and automates certain tasks, such as billing and scheduling, to operate more efficiently. They also offer new, specialized services to increase their competitive advantage and stand out in the market.

Building a strong leadership team: The company hires a new director of operations to oversee the growth process and ensure that all departments are working towards the same goals. The CEO also establishes a clear vision for the future of the business and communicates it to all employees.

Continuously innovating: The company invests in new technology to improve their services, such as a project management platform that makes communication with clients more efficient. They also explore new marketing strategies, such as targeted social media ads and email marketing campaigns.

By implementing these strategies, ABC Consulting is able to successfully scale and grow their business. They enter new markets, acquire new customers, and offer more specialized services, all while operating efficiently and remaining profitable. They are able to sustain this growth over time by continuing to innovate and adapt to changing market conditions.

Understanding the Stages of Business Growth

Starting a business can be an exciting, but also overwhelming process. To help entrepreneurs navigate through the different stages of business growth, it is important to understand the stages of business growth and the challenges that come with each stage. In this part , we will discuss the stages of business growth and the important considerations entrepreneurs should keep in mind as they grow their businesses.

The first stage of business growth is the start-up stage. During this stage, entrepreneurs are focused on getting their businesses off the ground. They are typically working on a shoestring budget, relying on their own personal resources and support from friends and family. At this stage, entrepreneurs are often focused on product development, market research, and establishing their brand.

The next stage of business growth is the growth stage. During this stage, the business has established a solid customer base and is beginning to grow its revenue and customer base. At this stage, entrepreneurs need to focus on scaling their operations, hiring employees, and investing in technology and other resources to support growth. This stage can also be a time of increased competition, so entrepreneurs need to focus on developing their brand and marketing efforts.

The third stage of business growth is the maturity stage. During this stage, the business has reached a level of stability and is generating consistent revenue. At this stage, entrepreneurs need to focus on maintaining their position in the market and ensuring their business remains profitable. This may involve investing in research and development, expanding into new markets, or developing new products and services.

The final stage of business growth is the decline stage. During this stage, the business may experience a decline in revenue, customer base, or market share. At this stage, entrepreneurs may need to make difficult decisions, such as closing down the business, selling it, or restructuring.

In conclusion, understanding the different stages of business growth is important for entrepreneurs as they navigate the ups and downs of starting and growing a business. By being aware of the challenges and opportunities that come with each stage, entrepreneurs can make informed decisions and increase their chances of success. Whether you are just starting out, or have been running your business for years, it is important to stay informed and continue learning to ensure you are on the right path to success.

Identifying Opportunities for Expansion

Identifying Opportunities for Expansion: A Key Component of Scaling Your Business

Expansion is a critical component of business growth and success, and it's essential for entrepreneurs to have a well-defined strategy for identifying and taking advantage of opportunities. In this article, we will explore the key aspects of identifying opportunities for expansion and how you can maximize your chances of success.

The first step in identifying opportunities for expansion is to conduct a thorough market analysis. This involves researching the current trends and demands in your industry, as well as assessing your competition. You should also evaluate your business's strengths and weaknesses, and identify areas where you can improve and expand.

Once you have a clear understanding of your market and competition, you should consider the various options available for expanding your business. This may include expanding into new markets, developing new products or services, or entering into strategic partnerships or collaborations.

It's also essential to stay up-to-date with emerging trends and technologies in your industry. This can help you identify new opportunities for growth and ensure that your business remains competitive. For example, if your business operates in the tech industry, you should stay informed about the latest advancements in artificial intelligence, the Internet of Things (IoT), and other relevant technologies.

Another important aspect of identifying opportunities for expansion is to have a strong network of contacts and advisors. This includes industry experts, business mentors, and professional organizations. These individuals and organizations can provide valuable insights and advice on emerging trends, as well as connect you with potential partners and investors.

Finally, it's crucial to be proactive in your approach to identifying opportunities for expansion. This means being open to new ideas and exploring different options, even if they are outside of your comfort zone. You should also be prepared to take calculated risks, as some of the most successful businesses have grown by taking bold and innovative steps.

In conclusion, identifying opportunities for expansion is a critical component of scaling your business. By conducting a thorough market analysis, staying informed about emerging trends, building a strong network of contacts, and being proactive in your approach, you can maximize your chances of success and ensure the continued growth of your business.

Building a Sustainable Business Model

Building a Sustainable Business Model: Essential for Long-Term Success

A sustainable business model is the cornerstone of long-term success for any business, regardless of its size or industry. A sustainable business model is one that not only generates revenue but also operates in a manner that is socially and environmentally responsible. In this part , we will explore the key elements of building a sustainable business model and how you can ensure the long-term success of your business.

The first step in building a sustainable business model is to identify and understand your target market. This involves conducting market research and analyzing the needs, preferences, and behavior of your target customers. Having a clear understanding of your target market will help you design and implement strategies that effectively meet their needs.

Once you have identified your target market, you should focus on developing a unique value proposition. This is the core of your business model and should clearly articulate the benefits that your customers will receive from your products or services. A unique value proposition will help you differentiate yourself from your competition and provide a compelling reason for customers to choose your business over others.

Another critical component of building a sustainable business model is to ensure that your operations are socially and environmentally responsible. This may involve implementing sustainable business practices, such as reducing your carbon footprint, using environmentally-friendly materials, or supporting local communities. By operating in a socially and environmentally responsible manner, you can not only benefit the planet but also enhance your brand reputation and attract more customers.

To further ensure the sustainability of your business, you should also focus on developing a strong financial foundation. This includes having a clear understanding of your financial statements, developing a robust budgeting and cash flow management plan, and seeking professional advice from financial advisors or accountants. A strong financial foundation will help you weather economic downturns and ensure that your business is able to sustain its operations for the long-term.

In conclusion, building a sustainable business model is essential for the long-term success of any business. By identifying and understanding your target market, developing a unique value proposition, operating in a socially and environmentally responsible manner, and ensuring a strong financial foundation, you can ensure the sustainability and growth of your business for many years to come.

Strategic Partnerships and Alliances

Strategic Partnerships and Alliances can play a crucial role in helping entrepreneurs grow and scale their businesses.

As an entrepreneur, forming strategic partnerships and alliances can be a game changer. By working with other businesses and organizations, entrepreneurs can access new resources, expertise, and markets that would otherwise be out of reach. However, it's essential to approach partnerships with a clear strategy and a well-defined plan to ensure that they are mutually beneficial and support the growth and success of the business.

One type of partnership that entrepreneurs can form is a joint venture. Joint ventures involve two or more businesses coming together to jointly pursue a specific project or opportunity. These partnerships can be particularly beneficial for entrepreneurs looking to access new markets, gain access to new customers, or leverage the expertise and resources of another organization.

Strategic partnerships are another type of partnership that entrepreneurs can form. These partnerships are more extensive and typically involve a long-term commitment between businesses to work together to achieve common goals. Strategic partnerships can provide entrepreneurs with a competitive advantage and help them overcome challenges by leveraging the expertise and resources of their partners.

Franchise arrangements are another type of partnership that entrepreneurs can explore. In a franchise arrangement, an entrepreneur licenses their business model and brand to another individual or organization, who then operates their own business using the franchisor's systems and processes. Franchise arrangements can help entrepreneurs expand their business quickly and efficiently while reducing the risk and costs associated with starting new businesses.

When forming partnerships and alliances, it's critical to identify potential partners carefully and build relationships based on trust and collaboration. Entrepreneurs should develop clear and defined goals and expectations, establish effective communication and negotiation strategies, and identify areas of complementarity between partners. This will help to ensure that partnerships are mutually beneficial and support the growth and success of the business.

It's also essential to monitor and evaluate partnerships regularly to ensure that they continue to support the growth and success of the business. This may involve making changes to the partnership agreement, adjusting goals and expectations, or even ending the partnership if it's no longer serving the best interests of the business.

In conclusion, strategic partnerships and alliances can play a crucial role in helping entrepreneurs grow and scale their businesses. By forming joint ventures, strategic partnerships, and franchise arrangements, entrepreneurs can access new resources, expertise, and markets, overcome challenges, and increase their chances of success. By approaching partnerships with a clear strategy, building relationships based on trust and collaboration, and monitoring and evaluating partnerships regularly, entrepreneurs can leverage partnerships to take their businesses to the next level and achieve their long-term goals.

International Expansion and Global Markets

International expansion and global markets is a critical component of scaling and growing a successful business. As entrepreneurs venture into new markets, they must be equipped to navigate the cultural, legal, and economic differences that exist in each country. Entrepreneurs must be strategic in their approach to entering new markets, as missteps can lead to significant financial losses.

In order to successfully expand into international markets, entrepreneurs must have a strong understanding of the key components of their business model and the resources required to scale their business globally. This includes identifying potential markets, understanding the target audience, and determining the best distribution channels. Entrepreneurs must also develop a thorough understanding of the local regulations, taxes, and legal requirements that apply to their business in each country.

Once the research has been completed, entrepreneurs must have the ability to make informed decisions about which markets to enter, how to structure their operations, and how to manage their resources effectively. This requires a deep understanding of their own capabilities, as well as an awareness of the competition in each market. Entrepreneurs must be able to pivot quickly if their initial strategies are not working and make key decisions that will drive their business forward.

In order to be successful in international markets, entrepreneurs must also be mindful of their impact on the local communities and environment. This includes ensuring that their operations are ethically and socially responsible, and that they are contributing to the local economy in a positive way. Entrepreneurs must be committed to their entrepreneurial ethics and social responsibility, as this will help to build trust with their customers and partners in new markets.

Finally, entrepreneurs must be prepared to continue learning and adapting as they expand into new markets. This requires a deep commitment to ongoing education and personal growth, as well as an open mind and a willingness to embrace change. By being agile, flexible, and proactive, entrepreneurs can successfully navigate the complexities of international expansion and succeed in new markets.

Leveraging Technology for Your Business

Leveraging technology for your business involves utilizing various technology tools and solutions to streamline your business operations, increase efficiency and productivity, and enhance customer experience. Here are some key concepts :

- Understanding the role of technology in business: This section could cover the importance of technology in today's business environment and how it can help businesses of all sizes to stay competitive.
- Identifying technologies that can benefit your business: Here, the focus could be on identifying the various technology tools and solutions that could be useful for your business, such as cloud computing, data analytics, social media, digital marketing, and more.
- Implementing and managing technology solutions: This section could provide practical advice on how to implement and manage technology solutions for your business, including the importance of cybersecurity, data privacy, and backup and recovery plans.
- Managing technology costs: As technology solutions can often come at a significant cost, it's important for entrepreneurs to understand how to manage their technology budgets and prioritize investments in technology tools and solutions.
- Integrating technology with business strategy: Finally, this section could cover how to align your technology strategy with your overall business strategy, to ensure that your technology investments are driving business growth and meeting customer needs.

Understanding the Role of Technology in Business

Understanding the role of technology in business is a crucial aspect of leveraging technology for your business. Here are some key concepts :

- Technology as an enabler of business success:
  The concept of technology as an enabler of business success refers to how technology has become an essential tool for modern business operations. This section could cover various aspects of how technology can help businesses to succeed, from managing finances to marketing and customer service. For instance, the use of accounting software can help businesses to manage their finances more efficiently and accurately, while digital marketing tools can help them to reach and engage with their target audience more effectively. Additionally, technology can enable businesses to offer more personalized and efficient customer service through the use of chatbots, customer relationship management (CRM) software, and other tools.
  Overall, understanding the role of technology as an enabler of business success is crucial for entrepreneurs who want to stay competitive in today's digital age. By leveraging technology solutions effectively, businesses can streamline their operations, enhance customer experiences, and ultimately achieve greater success and growth.

- Technology as a driver of innovation:
  The concept of technology as a driver of innovation refers to how technology has the power to spur new ideas, products, and services, and create new opportunities for entrepreneurs. This section could cover how technology has driven innovation in various industries, from e-commerce to healthcare, and how entrepreneurs

can leverage technology to create new products or services, enter new markets, or improve business processes.

For instance, the rise of e-commerce platforms such as Amazon and Alibaba has revolutionized the way people shop, and has created new opportunities for entrepreneurs to develop innovative products or services and reach new customers. In the healthcare industry, the development of new technologies such as telemedicine and health wearables has opened up new possibilities for delivering medical services and improving patient outcomes.

Overall, understanding the role of technology as a driver of innovation is crucial for entrepreneurs who want to stay ahead of the curve and remain competitive in their respective industries. By keeping up with the latest technological developments and leveraging them effectively, entrepreneurs can develop new and innovative solutions that meet the evolving needs of their customers and drive their businesses forward.

- Technology as a tool for collaboration and communication: With the increasing prevalence of remote work and global teams, technology tools can facilitate collaboration and communication across different teams, regions, and time zones. The concept of technology as a tool for collaboration and communication refers to how technology can help facilitate effective collaboration and communication among teams, even when they are geographically dispersed. technology tools can enable remote teams to work together effectively and efficiently, improving communication, coordination, and productivity.

  For instance, video conferencing tools like Zoom and Skype can enable team members to connect face-to-face, regardless of their location, while project management tools like Asana and Trello can help teams to track progress, set deadlines, and assign tasks. Additionally, cloud-based storage solutions like Google Drive and Dropbox can enable team members to access and share files and documents in real-time, regardless of their location.

  Overall, understanding the role of technology as a tool for collaboration and communication is essential for entrepreneurs who work with remote or geographically dispersed teams. By leveraging technology tools effectively, businesses can overcome the challenges of distance and time zones, and enable their teams to work together seamlessly and productively.

- Technology as a source of competitive advantage: Entrepreneurs who use technology to automate processes, gather and analyze data, and enhance customer experiences can often gain a competitive advantage over competitors who are slow to adopt technology solutions.

  The concept of technology as a source of competitive advantage refers to how businesses can leverage technology to gain an edge over their competitors.

  For instance, businesses can leverage automation technology to streamline their operations and reduce costs, enabling them to offer products or services at a lower price point. Additionally, businesses can use data analytics to gain insights into customer behavior, preferences, and trends, enabling them to develop more targeted and effective marketing strategies. By using technology to enhance the customer experience, businesses can also build stronger customer loyalty, increasing the likelihood of repeat business and positive word-of-mouth recommendations.

  Overall, understanding the role of technology as a source of competitive advantage is crucial for entrepreneurs who want to differentiate themselves from their competitors and gain a foothold in their respective markets. By leveraging technology solutions effectively, businesses can improve their efficiency, reduce costs, and offer better products or services, ultimately gaining an edge over their competitors and driving their growth and success.

- Technology as a means of improving efficiency and productivity:

  The concept of technology as a means of improving efficiency and productivity refers to how technology can help businesses optimize their operations, reduce costs, and improve overall efficiency and productivity. technology can help entrepreneurs to streamline routine tasks, automate processes, and free up time and resources to focus on strategic priorities and growth opportunities.

  For instance, businesses can leverage software tools to automate tasks such as data entry, inventory management, and accounting, reducing the time and resources required to perform these tasks manually. Additionally, businesses can use machine learning and artificial intelligence (AI) to identify inefficiencies and optimize their operations, improving their overall efficiency and productivity. By using technology to streamline their operations, businesses can also reduce costs, enabling them to offer products or services at a lower price point and remain competitive in their respective markets.

Overall, understanding the role of technology as a means of improving efficiency and productivity is essential for entrepreneurs who want to maximize their resources and drive their growth and success. By using technology solutions effectively, businesses can optimize their operations, reduce costs, and improve their overall efficiency and productivity, enabling them to focus on strategic priorities and pursue growth opportunities with greater speed and agility.

Identifying Technologies that can Benefit Your Business

Identifying technologies that can benefit your business involves understanding the range of technology tools and solutions that can help your business to become more efficient, effective, and competitive. Here are some key concepts :

- Cloud computing:
  Cloud computing is a technology solution that allows businesses to store and access data and applications remotely over the internet instead of on local servers or personal computers. By utilizing cloud computing, businesses can benefit from flexibility and scalability while also reducing costs associated with managing and maintaining physical hardware.
  Cloud computing services can be divided into three main categories: Infrastructure as a Service (IaaS), Platform as a Service (PaaS), and Software as a Service (SaaS). IaaS provides access to computing resources such as servers, storage, and networking, while PaaS offers a platform for building and deploying applications, and SaaS provides access to software applications hosted by third-party providers. Cloud computing solutions can provide businesses with a range of benefits, including the ability to access data and applications from anywhere, improved collaboration and communication, automatic updates and backups, and enhanced security. However, businesses must also consider the potential risks associated with using cloud computing, such as data breaches, downtime, and loss of control over data.

- Data analytics: Data analytics solutions enable businesses to collect, analyze, and gain insights from their data, which can inform decision-making, improve customer experiences, and identify new business opportunities.

Data analytics involves using technology tools to collect, process, and analyze large volumes of data in order to identify patterns, trends, and insights that can inform decision-making and improve business outcomes. By analyzing data, businesses can gain a deeper understanding of customer behaviors, market trends, and operational performance.

There are several types of data analytics, including descriptive, diagnostic, predictive, and prescriptive analytics. Descriptive analytics provides an overview of historical data, while diagnostic analytics seeks to identify the cause of specific events or trends. Predictive analytics uses statistical models and machine learning algorithms to forecast future events, and prescriptive analytics provides recommendations for future actions based on the insights gained from previous analyses.

Data analytics solutions can range from simple tools for data visualization and reporting to more complex software that incorporates machine learning algorithms and artificial intelligence. These solutions can be used across a range of business functions, from marketing and sales to finance and operations.

The benefits of using data analytics include improved decision-making, greater operational efficiency, and enhanced customer experiences. However, businesses must also consider potential challenges such as data quality, data privacy, and the need for skilled data analysts and IT professionals to manage and interpret data.

- Social media: Social media platforms offer a range of opportunities for businesses to connect with customers, promote products and services, and build brand awareness.

Social media platforms have become an essential part of businesses' marketing strategies, providing opportunities for companies to connect with customers, promote their products and services, and build brand awareness. Some popular social media platforms include Facebook, Instagram, Twitter, LinkedIn, and YouTube.

Through social media, businesses can engage with their target audience, sharing content such as blog posts, videos, images, and infographics that are relevant and valuable to their customers. Social media also allows businesses to interact with their customers in real-time, addressing their concerns and providing customer support.

In addition to organic reach, businesses can also use paid advertising on social media to target specific audiences and drive traffic to their websites or online stores. With the right targeting and messaging, social media advertising can be an effective way to generate leads, increase sales, and grow a business's customer base.

- Digital marketing: Digital marketing solutions, such as search engine optimization (SEO), pay-per-click (PPC) advertising, and email marketing, can help businesses to reach new audiences and increase sales.
Digital marketing refers to marketing activities that are conducted through digital channels, such as search engines, social media, email, and mobile apps. The goal of digital marketing is to reach and engage with potential customers online and convert them into paying customers.

Some common digital marketing strategies include:

- Search engine optimization (SEO): Optimizing a website's content and structure to improve its visibility in search engine results pages and increase organic traffic.
- Pay-per-click (PPC) advertising: Placing ads on search engine results pages or social media platforms and paying only when a user clicks on the ad.
- Email marketing: Sending promotional or informational emails to a list of subscribers who have opted in to receive them.
- Social media marketing: Using social media platforms to promote a business's products or services and engage with customers.
- Content marketing: Creating and sharing valuable, relevant, and consistent content to attract and retain a clearly defined audience.
Digital marketing is an effective way for businesses to reach a wider audience and drive more traffic to their websites or online stores. By leveraging data and analytics, businesses can optimize their digital marketing campaigns and improve their return on investment (ROI).
- Customer relationship management (CRM) software: CRM software solutions can help businesses to manage customer interactions, track sales leads, and build customer loyalty.

Customer relationship management (CRM) software is a technology tool that helps businesses to manage their interactions with customers, keep track of sales leads, and build customer loyalty. CRM software allows businesses to store customer data, such as contact information and purchase history, in a central database, which can be accessed and updated by different teams within the organization. By tracking customer interactions and preferences, businesses can personalize their marketing and sales efforts, improving the customer experience and increasing the likelihood of sales. CRM software can also help businesses to identify sales leads and track the progress of deals through the sales pipeline. Overall, CRM software can improve the efficiency and effectiveness of sales and marketing efforts, leading to increased customer satisfaction and revenue growth.

- E-commerce platforms:

E-commerce platforms are software solutions that enable businesses to sell products and services online. These platforms provide businesses with the ability to create online stores, list products, process payments, and manage orders and inventory. Some of the benefits of e-commerce platforms include:
- Increased sales: By offering products and services online, businesses can reach a wider audience and increase sales.
- Reduced costs: E-commerce platforms can help businesses reduce costs associated with traditional brick-and-mortar stores, such as rent, utilities, and staffing.
- 24/7 availability: E-commerce platforms provide customers with the ability to shop and make purchases at any time, increasing convenience and accessibility.
- Data and insights: E-commerce platforms provide businesses with access to valuable data and insights on customer behavior, preferences, and buying habits, which can inform business decisions and improve customer experiences.
- Integration with other tools: Many e-commerce platforms can integrate with other technology tools, such as payment gateways, shipping providers, and marketing automation software, providing businesses with a comprehensive solution for managing online sales
- Project management tools: Project management tools can help businesses to manage tasks, workflows, and teams, improving efficiency and productivity.

Project management tools can help businesses to plan, organize, and manage their projects effectively. These tools typically provide features for creating and assigning tasks, setting deadlines, tracking progress, and communicating with team members. By using project management tools, businesses can ensure that their projects are completed on time, within budget, and to a high standard of quality.

Some examples of popular project management tools include Trello, Asana, Jira, Basecamp, and Microsoft Project. These tools can be especially useful for businesses that have multiple teams or departments working on complex projects with many moving parts. By using a project management tool, all team members can stay informed about the status of the project, see what tasks they need to complete, and communicate with each other to ensure that everything is on track.

- Cybersecurity tools: Cybersecurity solutions, such as firewalls, antivirus software, and data encryption, can help businesses to protect their data and systems from cyber threats.

Cybersecurity tools refer to a variety of solutions that are used to protect computer systems and networks from unauthorized access, theft, and damage to data. These tools include hardware, software, and practices that aim to secure networks, devices, and data from cyber threats such as viruses, malware, and hacking attempts. Some common cybersecurity tools that can benefit businesses include firewalls, antivirus software, intrusion detection and prevention systems, data encryption, and security information and event management (SIEM) solutions. By implementing effective cybersecurity tools and practices, businesses can ensure the protection of their data, systems, and networks, and prevent potentially costly and damaging security breaches.

- Website and mobile app development tools: Website and mobile app development tools can help businesses to create digital platforms that provide intuitive and engaging user experiences.

Website and mobile app development tools enable businesses to create digital platforms that provide intuitive and engaging user experiences. Here are some key points to consider:
- Website development tools: There are a variety of website development tools available, ranging from drag-and-drop website builders to content management systems (CMS) like WordPress or Shopify. These tools can help businesses create a professional-looking website without requiring extensive coding knowledge or experience.
- Mobile app development tools: Mobile app development tools enable businesses to create custom mobile apps that provide customers with a seamless and convenient

user experience. There are a variety of tools available for businesses to develop mobile apps, such as Appy Pie, BuildFire, and Xamarin.

- User experience (UX) design: When developing a website or mobile app, it is important to consider the user experience (UX) design. This includes factors such as layout, navigation, and visual design. Good UX design can help to improve customer engagement and satisfaction.
- Responsive design: With an increasing number of users accessing websites and apps on mobile devices, it is important to ensure that your digital platforms are designed to be responsive to different screen sizes. This can be achieved through responsive design, which ensures that your website or app displays properly on a range of devices.
- Integration with other tools and services: Website and mobile app development tools often integrate with other tools and services, such as social media platforms, e-commerce solutions, and analytics tools. This can help businesses to streamline their operations and gain insights into customer behavior.
- Productivity and collaboration tools: Productivity and collaboration tools, such as video conferencing, instant messaging, and file-sharing software, can help businesses to communicate and work together more effectively, regardless of location.

Productivity and collaboration tools refer to software solutions that help businesses to improve communication, collaboration, and efficiency among team members. Here are some examples:

- Video conferencing software: Video conferencing software enables team members to hold virtual meetings and communicate face-to-face in real-time, regardless of their physical location.
- Instant messaging (IM) software: IM software allows team members to send messages to each other in real-time, improving communication and reducing the need for email communication.
- File-sharing software: File-sharing software allows team members to share and collaborate on documents, spreadsheets, and other files in real-time.
- Project management software: Project management software provides tools for planning, organizing, and managing projects, including task management, team collaboration, and progress tracking.
- Time-tracking software: Time-tracking software enables team members to track

their work hours and improve time management, which can increase productivity and efficiency.

- Workflow automation software: Workflow automation software helps businesses to automate routine tasks, reducing the need for manual intervention and improving efficiency.
- Virtual whiteboards: Virtual whiteboards allow team members to collaborate on brainstorming sessions and visualizing ideas, even if they are not in the same physical location.

Overall, these tools can help businesses to streamline communication, improve collaboration, and increase productivity, all of which can contribute to business success.

Implementing and Managing Technology Solutions

Implementing and managing technology solutions is an important aspect of leveraging technology for your business. Here are some key concepts :

- Assessing business needs: Before implementing any technology solutions, it is important to assess your business needs to ensure that the solutions you choose will align with your goals, priorities, and budget.
- Developing a technology strategy: A technology strategy is a roadmap that outlines how your business will use technology to achieve its goals. This section could cover how to create a technology strategy that is aligned with your business needs.
- Choosing technology solutions: This section could cover how to choose technology solutions that are the best fit for your business. It could also cover factors to consider when evaluating technology solutions, such as cost, functionality, ease of use, and scalability.
- Implementing technology solutions: This section could cover how to implement technology solutions effectively. It could include best practices for installation, testing, and training, as well as strategies for managing change and ensuring user adoption.
- Maintaining and upgrading technology solutions: Once technology solutions are implemented, it is important to maintain and upgrade them to ensure they continue to meet your business needs. This section could cover best practices for maintaining and upgrading technology solutions, including how to plan for updates and upgrades, how to manage downtime, and how to ensure data security during upgrades.
- Managing cybersecurity risks: As technology becomes more integrated into business operations, cybersecurity risks become more significant. This section

could cover how to identify and manage cybersecurity risks, including best practices for data protection, access control, and employee training.

- Measuring technology ROI: To determine the effectiveness of your technology solutions, it is important to measure their return on investment (ROI). This section could cover how to calculate ROI for technology solutions and how to use ROI data to inform technology strategy and investment decisions.
- Building a culture of innovation: Finally, implementing and managing technology solutions can help to build a culture of innovation within your business. This section could cover how to foster a culture of innovation, including best practices for encouraging experimentation, collaboration, and continuous learning.

Innovative and Sustainable Business Practices: Exploring New Ways to Build Businesses that Benefit People and the Planet

In today's world, businesses must not only focus on generating profits but also consider their impact on the environment and society. Companies that prioritize ethical and sustainable practices not only benefit the planet but also gain a competitive edge in the market. This is why the topic of innovative and sustainable business practices is of utmost importance to entrepreneurs who wish to create successful and impactful ventures.

What are Innovative and Sustainable Business Practices?

Innovative and sustainable business practices refer to the methods and strategies adopted by companies to reduce their negative impact on the environment, society, and economy while maximizing their positive impact. This involves taking into account the entire lifecycle of a product or service, from production to disposal, and ensuring that it is designed, manufactured, and delivered in a way that is environmentally friendly and socially responsible.

Importance of sustainable practices

Why are Innovative and Sustainable Business Practices important?

Businesses have a significant impact on the world around them, and their practices can either contribute to or detract from the well-being of society and the planet. Innovative and sustainable business practices are important for several reasons:

1. Social Responsibility: Companies have a responsibility to operate in a way that benefits society, including their employees, customers, and the wider community. By adopting sustainable practices, businesses can reduce their negative impact on society and contribute to positive change.
2. Competitive Advantage: Companies that prioritize sustainability and innovation gain a competitive advantage in the market. Consumers are increasingly aware of the environmental and social impact of the products they purchase and are more likely to support companies that align with their values.
3. Long-Term Viability: Businesses that prioritize sustainability are more likely to be successful in the long term. This is because they are better able to adapt to changing market conditions, reduce costs, and attract and retain employees who share their values.
4. Environmental Protection: The planet is facing unprecedented environmental challenges, including climate change, pollution, and loss of biodiversity. Businesses that adopt sustainable practices can help to mitigate these challenges by reducing their carbon footprint, conserving natural resources, and minimizing waste.

There are several reasons why innovative and sustainable business practices are important. First and foremost, companies have a responsibility to operate in a way that benefits society, including their employees, customers, and the wider community. By adopting sustainable practices, businesses can reduce their negative impact on society and contribute to positive change. In addition, companies that prioritize sustainability and innovation gain a competitive adv antage in the market. Consumers are increasingly aware of the environmental and social impact of the products they purchase and are more likely to support companies that align with their values. Furthermore, businesses that prioritize sustainability are more likely to be successful in the long term. This is because they are better able to adapt to changing market conditions, reduce costs, and attract and retain employees who share their values. Finally, businesses that adopt sustainable practices can help to mitigate environmental challenges by reducing their carbon footprint, conserving natural resources, and minimizing waste.

There are many ways that businesses can adopt innovative and sustainable practices. One way is to switch to renewable energy sources, such as solar or wind power, for their operations. This can help to reduce a company's carbon footprint. Another way is to use sustainable packaging materials, such as biodegradable or compostable materials, in order to reduce waste. Companies can also reduce waste and conserve resources by recycling materials or repurposing them for other uses. Additionally, businesses can ensure that their products are produced in an ethical and sustainable manner by sourcing materials from suppliers who meet certain standards. Finally, companies can engage their employees in sustainability initiatives by providing training and resources to help them reduce their environmental impact both in the workplace and at home.

Examples of Innovative and Sustainable Business Practices

There are many ways that businesses can adopt innovative and sustainable practices. Here are a few examples:
1. Renewable Energy: Companies can reduce their carbon footprint by switching to renewable energy sources, such as solar or wind power, for their operations.
2. Sustainable Packaging: Businesses can reduce waste by using sustainable packaging materials, such as biodegradable or compostable materials.
3. Recycling and Upcycling: Companies can reduce waste and conserve resources by recycling materials or repurposing them for other uses.
4. Ethical Sourcing: Businesses can ensure that their products are produced in an ethical and sustainable manner by sourcing materials from suppliers who meet certain standards.
5. Employee Engagement: Companies can engage their employees in sustainability initiatives by providing training and resources to help them reduce their environmental impact both in the workplace and at home.

Challenges to Implementing Innovative and Sustainable Business Practices

While there are many benefits to adopting innovative and sustainable business practices, there are also several challenges that businesses may face:

Cost: Implementing sustainable practices can require significant upfront investment, which may be a challenge for businesses with limited resources. This investment may include the cost of new equipment, technology, or materials, as well as the cost of training employees to use these new tools. While sustainable practices can result in long-term cost savings and increased efficiency, businesses may struggle to justify these initial costs without a clear understanding of the potential benefits.

Resistance to Change: Some employees or stakeholders may be resistant to change, particularly if they perceive sustainability initiatives as adding additional work or inconvenience. They may also not understand the benefits of sustainable practices or may not see how these practices align with the company's goals. Addressing this challenge may require clear communication and education about the benefits of sustainability, as well as involving employees in the development and implementation of sustainable practices.

Lack of Expertise: Implementing sustainable practices often requires specialized knowledge or expertise that may not exist within the company. Without this knowledge, businesses may struggle to implement sustainable practices effectively or may make mistakes that lead to unintended consequences. Addressing this challenge may require partnering with external experts or investing in employee training and development.

Regulatory Environment: Some countries or regions may have regulations or policies that make it difficult for businesses to adopt sustainable practices. For example, regulations may limit the use of certain materials or technologies, or may impose additional costs or requirements on businesses that want to adopt sustainable practices. Addressing this challenge may require working with policymakers and regulatory bodies to create more supportive policies or finding ways to comply with existing regulations in a sustainable way.

Lack of Consumer Demand: While sustainability is becoming increasingly important to consumers, there may still be a lack of demand for sustainable products or services in some markets. Businesses may struggle to justify the costs of sustainability initiatives if they don't see a corresponding increase in sales or customer loyalty. Addressing this challenge may require educating consumers about the benefits of sustainability or finding creative ways to increase demand for sustainable products and services.

Overcoming the Challenges of Implementing Innovative and Sustainable Business Practices

While there are challenges to implementing innovative and sustainable business practices, there are also solutions that businesses can adopt to overcome them. Here are a few examples:

Cost: While implementing sustainable practices may require upfront investment, it can also result in long-term cost savings. For example, reducing energy consumption through the use of renewable energy sources or improving the efficiency of operations can lead to significant cost savings over time. Additionally, businesses can explore funding opportunities or partnerships with government agencies or non-profit organizations that support sustainable initiatives.

Resistance to Change: To overcome resistance to change, businesses can communicate the benefits of sustainable practices and involve employees and stakeholders in the decision-making process. Providing training and resources to help employees understand the importance of sustainability can also be effective in overcoming resistance.

Lack of Expertise: Businesses can overcome the lack of expertise by hiring consultants or experts in sustainable practices or by partnering with organizations that specia lize in sustainable initiatives. Additionally, businesses can provide training and resources to employees to help build their knowledge and skills in sustainability.

Regulatory Environment: While regulations can be a challenge, they can also provide incentives for businesses to adopt sustainable practices. Businesses can stay informed about regulatory changes and work with government agencies or industry associations to advocate for policies that support sustainability.

Lack of Consumer Demand: While consumer demand for sustainable products and services may be lacking in some markets, businesses can take steps to educate consumers about the benefits of sustainability and build awareness around their own sustainable practices. Additionally, businesses can work with industry associations or non-profit organizations to build demand for sustainable products and services.

To overcome these challenges, businesses must be committed to sustainable practices and prioritize them in their operations. They can start by conducting a sustainability assessment to identify areas where they can reduce their environmental impact and increase their social responsibility. They can also engage their employees and stakeholders in sustainability initiatives and provide them with the resources and training they need to implement sustainable practices effectively. Furthermore, companies can collaborate with other organizations and industry groups to share best practices and collaborate on sustainability initiatives. Finally, businesses can work with governments and policymakers to advocate for policies that support sustainable practices and make it easier for companies to adopt them.

Innovative and sustainable business practices are essential for businesses that wish to create successful and impactful ventures. These practices can help to reduce a company's negative impact on the environment and society while maximizing its positive impact. While there are challenges to implementing sustainable practices, businesses must be committed to them in order to succeed in the long term. By prioritizing sustainability, companies can gain a competitive advantage in the market, reduce costs, and attract and retain employees who share their values.

Conclusion

Innovative and sustainable business practices are essential for creating successful and impactful ventures in today's world. By adopting sustainable practices, businesses can reduce their negative impact on the environment and society, gain a competitive advantage in the market, and contribute to positive change. While there are challenges to implementing sustainable practices, there are also solutions that businesses can adopt to overcome them. By prioritizing sustainability and innovation, businesses can build a more sustainable and prosperous future for themselves and for the world around them.

Balancing Work and Life as an Entrepreneur

Balancing work and life is a crucial aspect of maintaining mental and emotional health as an entrepreneur. Here are some key concepts:

- Setting boundaries: One of the most important steps in achieving work-life balance is setting clear boundaries between work and personal life. This section could cover how to set boundaries, such as creating a designated workspace, setting specific work hours, and avoiding work-related activities outside of those hours.

- Prioritizing self-care: It can be easy for entrepreneurs to prioritize work over self-care, but neglecting self-care can have serious negative consequences. This section could cover how to prioritize self-care, such as getting enough sleep, exercise, and social support.

- Delegating and outsourcing: Entrepreneurs often feel like they need to do everything themselves, but delegating and outsourcing can be an effective way to free up time and reduce stress. This section could cover how to identify tasks that can be delegated or outsourced, as well as how to find reliable contractors or employees to handle those tasks.

- Time management: Effective time management is key to balancing work and life as an entrepreneur. This section could cover time-management strategies, such as prioritizing tasks, using productivity tools, and setting realistic deadlines.

- Building a support network: Building a support network is important for both personal and professional growth. This section could cover how to build a network of peers, mentors, and friends who can offer support, guidance, and feedback.

- Fostering work-life integration: Work-life integration is an alternative to work-life balance that involves finding ways to blend work and personal life in a way that feels fulfilling and sustainable. This section could cover how to foster work-life integration, such as by setting flexible work hours, incorporating personal interests into work activities, and finding ways to use work skills to contribute to personal goals.

- Managing stress and burnout: Entrepreneurs are at high risk of burnout due to the demands and pressures of starting and running a business. This section could cover how to identify signs of stress and burnout, as well as how to manage those symptoms, such as through stress reduction techniques, seeking professional help, and taking breaks when needed.
- Reflecting on values and goals: Finally, balancing work and life requires a deep understanding of personal values and goals. This section could cover how to reflect on and clarify

The operation couldn't be completed. (kCFErrorDomainCFNetwork error 303.) personal values and goals, as well as how to align work activities with those values and goals in order to achieve a sense of purpose and fulfillment. This could involve exercises such as journaling, meditation, or talking to a mentor or coach.

Understanding the Importance of Work-Life Balance

Understanding the importance of work-life balance is crucial for the success and well-being of entrepreneurs. Here are some key concepts :

- Promoting mental and emotional health: Maintaining a healthy work-life balance is essential for promoting good mental and emotional health. This section could cover how overworking and neglecting personal life can lead to stress, burnout, and other negative consequences, and how prioritizing personal well-being can lead to increased productivity and better business outcomes.
- Increasing productivity and creativity: Working long hours without breaks can lead to decreased productivity and creativity. This section could cover how taking regular breaks and having a healthy work-life balance can lead to increased focus, creativity, and efficiency.
- Improving relationships: Entrepreneurs who prioritize work over personal life risk damaging important relationships with family, friends, and romantic partners. This section could cover how balancing work and personal life can lead to stronger relationships and a more fulfilling personal life.
- Avoiding burnout: Burnout is a common problem for entrepreneurs who work long hours and neglect self-care. This section could cover how balancing work and personal life can help entrepreneurs avoid burnout and maintain the energy and passion needed to run a successful business.
- Attracting and retaining talent: Employees are increasingly seeking work-life balance as a key component of a fulfilling career. This section could cover how prioritizing work-life balance can help entrepreneurs attract and retain top talent, as well as promote a positive company culture.
- Achieving long-term success: Achieving long-term success requires sustainable practices, including a healthy work-life balance. This section could cover how

entrepreneurs who prioritize work-life balance are more likely to achieve long-term success and sustainability, as well as how balancing work and personal life can lead to a sense of purpose and fulfillment.

Strategies for Managing Work and Personal Life

Strategies for managing work and personal life are critical for entrepreneurs who want to maintain a healthy balance between their professional and personal lives. Here are some strategies :

- Establishing boundaries: Setting clear boundaries between work and personal life is essential for maintaining a healthy work-life balance. This section could cover how entrepreneurs can set boundaries by establishing designated work hours, separating work and personal devices, and limiting work-related communication outside of work hours.
- Prioritizing self-care: Prioritizing self-care is an important strategy for managing work and personal life. This section could cover how entrepreneurs can prioritize self-care by scheduling regular breaks, engaging in physical exercise, practicing mindfulness, and taking vacations.
- Delegating and outsourcing: Delegating and outsourcing tasks can help entrepreneurs manage their workload and focus on higher-level tasks. This section could cover how entrepreneurs can delegate tasks to employees or outsource work to freelancers or contractors to free up time for personal life activities.
- Managing time effectively: Managing time effectively is critical for entrepreneurs who want to balance work and personal life. This section could cover strategies such as time blocking, prioritizing tasks, and eliminating distractions to help entrepreneurs make the most of their time.
- Creating a support system: Creating a support system is an important strategy for managing work and personal life. This section could cover how entrepreneurs can build a network of supportive friends, family members, and colleagues who can offer emotional and practical support during times of stress or overload.

- Managing expectations: Managing expectations is essential for reducing stress and maintaining a healthy work-life balance. This section could cover how entrepreneurs can manage expectations by communicating clearly with clients, employees, and stakeholders about work hours, project timelines, and personal commitments.

By implementing these strategies, entrepreneurs can more effectively manage their work and personal lives, reduce stress, and achieve a healthier work-life balance.

Developing Habits for Maintaining Well-being and Health

Developing habits for maintaining well-being and health is important for entrepreneurs who want to stay healthy and productive. Here are some habits :
- Prioritizing sleep: Getting enough quality sleep is crucial for maintaining good health and productivity. This section could cover the importance of sleep and offer strategies for developing healthy sleep habits, such as sticking to a regular sleep schedule, creating a relaxing sleep environment, and avoiding screens before bedtime.
- Eating a balanced diet: Eating a balanced diet is essential for maintaining good health and energy levels. This section could cover the importance of good nutrition and offer tips for developing healthy eating habits, such as eating a variety of whole foods, limiting processed foods, and avoiding sugary drinks.
- Exercising regularly: Regular exercise is important for maintaining physical and mental health. This section could cover the benefits of exercise and offer strategies for developing a regular exercise routine, such as finding an activity that you enjoy, setting achievable fitness goals, and incorporating exercise into your daily routine.
- Practicing mindfulness: Practicing mindfulness is a helpful habit for managing stress and maintaining good mental health. This section could cover the benefits of mindfulness and offer tips for developing a mindfulness practice, such as meditation, deep breathing, or practicing gratitude.
- Taking breaks and practicing self-care: Taking regular breaks and practicing self-care is important for maintaining well-being and preventing burnout. This section could cover the benefits of taking breaks and offer tips for developing self-care habits, such as scheduling regular breaks throughout the day, taking time off for hobbies and personal interests, and engaging in activities that bring joy.
- Seeking professional support: Seeking professional support is important for

maintaining good health and addressing health issues as they arise. This section could cover the importance of seeking professional support, such as visiting a doctor or mental health professional when needed.

By implementing these habits, entrepreneurs can maintain good health and well-

Ethics and Social Responsibility in Entrepreneurship

Ethics and social responsibility are important considerations for entrepreneurs, who have the potential to impact their communities and society as a whole. Here are some topics :

- Understanding the importance of ethics and social responsibility:
  Entrepreneurs play an important role in shaping society, and their decisions can have significant impacts on their stakeholders. Ethics and social responsibility are important considerations for entrepreneurs, as they help to ensure that businesses are operating in a way that benefits society as a whole, rather than just their own interests. Ethical business practices can help to build trust with customers, employees, investors, and other stakeholders, which can lead to long-term success. Social responsibility involves taking actions that go beyond simply complying with laws and regulations, and instead focus on making a positive impact on society and the environment. By considering ethics and social responsibility in their business decisions, entrepreneurs can build a strong reputation and create value for all stakeholders.

- Developing a code of ethics:
  A code of ethics is a document that outlines the values and principles that a company follows in its operations. It can help entrepreneurs to establish a clear set of guidelines for ethical decision-making and communicate their values to stakeholders. The process of developing a code of ethics should involve input from all stakeholders, including employees, customers, suppliers, and investors. The code should include key elements such as honesty, transparency, respect, and responsibility. It is important to communicate the code of ethics clearly to all employees and stakeholders, and to regularly review and update it as needed. Enforcement mechanisms such as regular training and monitoring can also help to ensure that the code is being followed.

- Incorporating social responsibility into business practices:
  There are many ways in which entrepreneurs can incorporate social responsibility into their business practices. Some examples include using sustainable materials and processes, reducing waste and carbon emissions, supporting local communities through donations or volunteer work, and implementing fair labor practices. Social responsibility can also involve engaging with stakeholders to understand their needs and concerns, and taking action to address them. By incorporating social responsibility into their business practices, entrepreneurs can create a positive impact on society and the environment, and differentiate themselves from competitors.

- Balancing ethical considerations with business goals:
  Entrepreneurs may face challenges in balancing ethical considerations with their business goals. This can involve making difficult decisions that balance the needs of different stakeholders, such as customers, employees, investors, and the broader society. One strategy for making ethical decisions is to consider the impact of business decisions on all stakeholders, and to use ethical frameworks such as utilitarianism or deontology to guide decision-making. Seeking advice from trusted advisors, such as mentors or ethical experts, can also be helpful in making difficult ethical decisions. By balancing ethical considerations with business goals, entrepreneurs can build a reputation as a socially responsible business and create long-term value for all stakeholders.

- Responding to ethical challenges and dilemmas:
  Entrepreneurs may face ethical challenges and dilemmas in the course of their business. It is important to address these issues promptly and transparently, and to seek input from all stakeholders to understand the impact of the issue. Taking responsibility for mistakes and making amends can also help to rebuild trust with stakeholders. One strategy for responding to ethical challenges is to have a crisis management plan in place, which outlines the steps to take in the event of a crisis or ethical challenge. By responding to ethical challenges in a responsible and transparent way, entrepreneurs can demonstrate their commitment to ethical business practices and build trust with stakeholders

Understanding the Role of Ethics and
Social Responsibility in Business

Ethics and social responsibility are key considerations in modern business. Ethics refers to the principles and values that guide individual and organizational behavior, while social responsibility refers to the impact of an organization's actions on society and the environment.

Understanding the role of ethics and social responsibility in business is important for several reasons. First, ethical behavior can help build trust with customers and other stakeholders, which is essential for long-term success. Second, social responsibility is increasingly important for companies as consumers become more aware of the environmental and social impact of their purchases. Third, ethical and socially responsible behavior can help companies attract and retain talented employees who are motivated by more than just financial incentives.

Businesses have a responsibility to consider the impact of their actions on society and the environment. This can involve taking steps to reduce their environmental footprint, supporting community initiatives, and providing fair and safe working conditions for employees. Companies that prioritize ethics and social responsibility can build strong relationships with customers, suppliers, and other stakeholders, which can lead to long-term success.

In addition to its importance for individual businesses, ethics and social responsibility are also becoming more important for the global economy. As issues such as climate change and income inequality continue to attract attention, consumers and investors are looking to businesses to take a leadership role in addressing these challenges. By prioritizing ethics and social responsibility, businesses can help to create a more sustainable and equitable future for all.

Identifying Ethical and Social Responsibilities in Your Business

Identifying ethical and social responsibilities in your business is an important step in building a sustainable and successful enterprise. Here are some steps to help you identify these responsibilities:

- Conduct a stakeholder analysis: Identify the key stakeholders in your business, such as customers, employees, suppliers, and the community. Consider their interests and needs, and how your business impacts them.
- Review your mission and values: Look at your company's mission statement and values to determine if they align with ethical and social responsibility goals.
- Evaluate your operations: Evaluate your business practices and identify areas where you could improve your ethical and social responsibility. For example, you may need to improve working conditions, reduce waste and emissions, or increase diversity and inclusion.
- Research industry standards and regulations: Research your industry's standards and regulations regarding ethical and social responsibility. Ensure that your business is compliant with these standards and regulations.
- Solicit feedback: Ask for feedback from your employees, customers, and other stakeholders to identify areas where your business can improve its ethical and social responsibility.
- Develop a plan: Once you have identified the key areas of responsibility, develop a plan to address them. Set specific goals and timelines for implementation, and regularly review and update your plan.

By identifying and addressing ethical and social responsibilities, your business can build stronger relationships with stakeholders, attract and retain employees, and contribute to a more sustainable and equitable future.

Incorporating Ethics and Social Responsibility into Your Business Practices

Incorporating ethics and social responsibility into your business practices is a vital step in building a sustainable and socially responsible enterprise. Here are some strategies to help you incorporate ethics and social responsibility into your business practices:

- Develop a code of ethics: A code of ethics outlines the ethical principles and values that guide your business practices. It can help your employees understand the importance of ethical behavior and hold themselves accountable.
- Integrate sustainability practices: Identify areas where your business can reduce its environmental impact, such as reducing waste, conserving energy, and using sustainable materials. This can help improve your business's environmental sustainability and contribute to a more sustainable future.
- Foster a culture of diversity and inclusion: Create an inclusive workplace culture that embraces diversity and promotes equal opportunities for all employees. Encourage open communication, collaboration, and respect for different perspectives and experiences.
- Give back to the community: Find ways to give back to the community, such as through volunteering, charitable donations, or supporting local businesses. This can help your business build strong relationships with your community and demonstrate your commitment to social responsibility.
- Ensure fair treatment of employees and suppliers: Develop policies and practices that ensure fair treatment of employees and suppliers. This includes providing fair compensation, ensuring safe working conditions, and complying with labor laws.
- Regularly evaluate and update your practices: Regularly evaluate your business practices to ensure they align with your ethical and social responsibility goals.

Update your policies and practices as needed to ensure your business remains socially responsible and sustainable.

By incorporating ethics and social responsibility into your business practices, you can build a strong reputation and establish trust with your customers, employees, and stakeholders. This can help your business succeed over the long term and contribute to a more sustainable and equitable future.

Conclusion and Final Thoughts

Conclusion and Final Thoughts: Reflecting on Your Entrepreneurial Journey

Starting and growing a successful business is a challenging but rewarding journey. It requires hard work, dedication, and a commitment to making your dreams a reality. As you reach the conclusion of your entrepreneurial journey, it's essential to reflect on what you've accomplished and the lessons you've learned along the way. In this article, we'll explore the significance of conclusion and final thoughts and how to reflect on your entrepreneurial journey.

Firstly, it's crucial to celebrate your accomplishments. As an entrepreneur, it's easy to get caught up in the day-to-day grind and overlook your achievements. However, taking the time to acknowledge and celebrate your successes, no matter how big or small, is important in maintaining a positive outlook and motivation to continue growing your business.

Another important aspect of conclusion and final thoughts is to reflect on what you've learned. Entrepreneurship is a continuous learning experience, and reflecting on the lessons you've learned can help you grow both personally and professionally. Consider the challenges you've faced, the decisions you've made, and the results you've achieved. Take the time to identify what worked well and what didn't, and use these lessons to inform future decisions and strategies.

Lastly, it's essential to encourage continued learning and growth. As your business evolves, so should your skills and knowledge. Staying up to date with industry trends and developments and seeking out opportunities to learn and grow will help you stay ahead of the competition and maintain a competitive edge.

In conclusion, the conclusion and final thoughts of your entrepreneurial journey are a crucial time for reflection, celebration, and growth. By taking the time to acknowledge your accomplishments, reflect on your lessons learned, and encourage continued learning and growth, you'll be well on your way to continued success and the realization of your entrepreneurial dreams.

Reflecting on Your Entrepreneurial Journey

Reflecting on Your Entrepreneurial Journey: The Importance of Self-Reflection in Entrepreneurship

Starting and growing a business is a challenging and rewarding journey. As an entrepreneur, it's essential to take the time to reflect on your journey and celebrate your accomplishments, no matter how big or small.

Firstly, reflecting on your journey helps you to identify areas for improvement. As you reflect on your experiences, it's easier to identify areas where you excelled, as well as areas where you struggled. By recognizing areas for improvement, you can focus on developing your skills and knowledge and make better decisions in the future.

Secondly, reflecting on your journey allows you to acknowledge your accomplishments. As an entrepreneur, it's easy to get caught up in the day-to-day grind and overlook your achievements. However, taking the time to acknowledge and celebrate your successes, no matter how big or small, is important in maintaining a positive outlook and motivation to continue growing your business.

Thirdly, reflecting on your journey can help you build resilience and adaptability. Entrepreneurship is full of challenges and obstacles, and reflecting on how you overcame them can help you develop the resilience and adaptability you need to succeed.

Finally, reflecting on your journey can help you identify patterns and trends. By taking the time to reflect on your experiences and the decisions you've made, you can identify patterns and trends in your behavior and decision-making processes. This information can help you make better decisions in the future and increase your chances of success.

In conclusion, reflecting on your entrepreneurial journey is a crucial aspect of personal and professional growth. By taking the time to reflect on your experiences, acknowledge your accomplishments, build resilience, and identify patterns and trends, you'll be well on your way to continued success and the realization of your entrepreneurial dreams.

Celebrating Your Accomplishments

It's essential to celebrate your accomplishments, no matter how big or small.

Firstly, celebrating your accomplishments helps to boost your confidence and motivation. When you take the time to acknowledge and celebrate your successes, you'll feel more confident and motivated to continue working towards your goals. Recognizing your achievements can also increase your sense of pride and fulfillment, helping to boost your overall well-being.

Secondly, celebrating your accomplishments can help you build a positive work-life balance. When you're working hard to grow your business, it's easy to get caught up in the day-to-day grind and forget to take time for yourself. Celebrating your successes gives you an opportunity to take a step back, recharge, and enjoy the fruits of your labor.

Thirdly, celebrating your accomplishments helps to foster a positive company culture. When you celebrate your successes as a team, it can help to build a positive and supportive work environment, increase employee morale, and foster a sense of collaboration and teamwork.

Finally, celebrating your accomplishments helps to establish a pattern of success. When you take the time to celebrate your successes, you'll develop a habit of recognizing and appreciating your achievements. This habit can help you stay motivated and focused on your goals, even when faced with challenges and obstacles.

In conclusion, celebrating your accomplishments is an essential aspect of personal and professional growth in entrepreneurship. By taking the time to recognize and appreciate your successes, you'll boost your confidence, build a positive work-life balance, foster a positive company culture, and establish a pattern of success. So, make sure to take the time to celebrate your achievements, no matter how big or small, and continue working towards the realization of your entrepreneurial dreams.

Encouraging Continued Learning and Growth

Encouraging Continued Learning and Growth: The Key to Success in Entrepreneurship

Entrepreneurship is a journey of continuous learning and growth. The business landscape is constantly evolving, and it's essential for entrepreneurs to stay up-to-date with the latest trends, strategies, and technologies to stay competitive and achieve success.

Firstly, continued learning and growth can help you stay ahead of the curve. Entrepreneurs who invest in their education and skills development are better equipped to navigate the challenges and opportunities of a rapidly changing business environment. By staying informed about industry trends and advancements, you'll be better positioned to make informed decisions and capitalize on emerging opportunities.

Secondly, continued learning and growth can help you remain innovative and creative. Entrepreneurs who invest in their education and professional development are better equipped to develop new ideas, approaches, and solutions to business problems. By challenging yourself to learn new things, you'll foster your creativity and remain at the forefront of innovation in your industry.

Thirdly, continued learning and growth can help you build a more successful business. Entrepreneurs who invest in their education and skills development are better equipped to build a more successful and sustainable business. By acquiring new knowledge and skills, you'll be better equipped to make informed decisions, develop more effective strategies, and build a stronger team.

Finally, continued learning and growth can help you achieve greater personal fulfillment. Entrepreneurs who invest in their education and professional development are more likely to experience a greater sense of personal fulfillment and satisfaction. By challenging yourself to learn new things, you'll not only build a more successful business, but you'll also grow and develop as an individual.

In conclusion, encouraging continued learning and growth is a critical aspect of success in entrepreneurship. By investing in your education and professional development, you'll stay ahead of the curve, remain innovative and creative, build a more successful business, and achieve greater personal fulfillment. So, make sure to prioritize continued learning and growth in your entrepreneurial journey, and you'll be well on your way to realizing your entrepreneurial dreams.

Epilogue

In conclusion, "Fuel Your Dreams: A Guide to Fueling Entrepreneurship" has provided you with a comprehensive overview of the key concepts and strategies for successful entrepreneurship. From identifying and validating your business idea, to securing funding and investment, to building a strong team, to marketing and branding, to managing your finances, and navigating challenges and overcoming obstacles, this book has covered it all.

We hope that you've found the information and guidance provided in this book to be valuable and inspiring, and that you've gained the knowledge and confidence needed to turn your entrepreneurial dreams into a reality.

Remember, entrepreneurship is a journey of continuous learning and growth, and we encourage you to continue to seek out new knowledge, skills, and opportunities that will help you succeed. Celebrate your accomplishments, reflect on your journey, and always be open to learning and growth, and you'll be well on your way to achieving your entrepreneurial dreams.

So, go out there and fuel your dreams!

The world is waiting for your entrepreneurial spirit and vision.

sincerely
 Ehsan Zarrini Darban